Optimal stop and line spacing for urban public transport networks
Analysis of objectives and implications for planning practice

TRAIL Studies in Transportation Science

International Editorial Council:

    Prof.dr.-Eng. Hideo Nakamura
    Institute for Transport Policy Studies, Tokyo, Japan

    Prof. Avishai Ceder
    Technion, Haifa, Israel

    Prof.dr.-ing. Werner Brilon
    Ruhr University, Bochum, Germany

Optimal stop and line spacing for urban public transport networks
Analysis of objectives and implications for planning practice

TRAIL Research School

Author:

ir. Rob van Nes
Transportation Section
Faculty of Civil Engineering and Geosciences, Delft University of Technology

TRAIL Studies in Transportation Science N°. S2000/01

Editor: Prof.dr.ir. P.H.L. Bovy

Editorial board: Prof.dr.-ing. I.A. Hansen
Prof.dr.ir. R.E.C.M. van der Heijden
Prof.dr. G.J. Olsder
Prof.ir. F.M. Sanders

The Netherlands TRAIL Research School
Delft University of Technology
Erasmus University Rotterdam
University of Groningen

TRAIL-office
Kluyverweg 4
P.O. Box 5017
2600 GA Delft
The Netherlands
Telephone : +31 (0) 15 278 60 46
Telefax : +31 (0) 15 278 43 33
E-mail : mailbox@TRAIL.tudelft.nl
Internet : www.TRAIL.tudelft.nl

Sales and distribution:
Delft University Press
P.O. Box 98
2600 MG Delft
Telephone: +31 (0)15 278 32 54
Telefax: +31 (0)15 278 16 61

ISBN: 90-407-2081-9

© Copyright by The Netherlands TRAIL Research School. No part of this book may be reproduced in any form by print, photoprint, microfilm or any other means without written permission of the publisher: The Netherlands TRAIL Research School.

TRAIL is accredited by the Royal Netherlands Academy of Arts and Sciences and is a co-operative venture in which seven faculties of the **Delft University of Technology** participate: Civil Engineering and Geosciences (CEG), Design, Engineering and Production (DEP), Architecture (ARC), Information Technology & Systems (ITS), Aerospace Engineering (AE), Technology, Policy & Management (TPM), Applied Sciences and OTB Research Institute for Housing, Urban and Mobility studies; four faculties of the **Erasmus University of Rotterdam**: Economic Sciences (FES), Business Administration (FBA), Social Sciences (FSS) and Law (FL), and one faculty of the ***University* of Groningen**: Behavioural and Social Sciences (BSS).

Preface

This publication is a result of the research program "Seamless Multimodal Mobility" carried out within The Netherlands TRAIL Research School for Transport, Infrastructure and Logistics, and financed by the Delft University of Technology.

The "Seamless Multimodal Mobility" research program will provide tools for the design and operation of attractive and efficient multimodal personal transport services. This report presents results of a study that is part of project 2 "Design theory for mixed multimodal networks". The objective of project 2 is to develop theories and techniques to design multimodal transport service networks and multimodal transfer points. The focus in this report is on transport network design only.

In the report "Design of multimodal transport systems, Setting the scene, Review of literature and basic concepts" (Van Nes (1999)) it is concluded that interurban transport networks appear to be robust, that is, they are strongly dependent on spatial structures. Urban public transport service networks, on the other hand, might be more flexible and might be optimised. In this report the focus is on the latter subject, optimisation of urban public transport service networks, and especially on the key design variables of an urban public transport network: stop spacing and line spacing. The objective of this report is to present a broad view on this subject: review of literature, description of modelling characteristics, impact of objectives and assumptions, and implications for planning practice.

Finally, the author would like to thank Arjen Bos for analysing current urban public transport networks, Kaspar Koolstra and Ulrich Schäffeler for their ideas and discussions, and especially Piet Bovy for his suggestions and advice.

Summary

Stop spacing and line spacing are key design variables for an urban public transport service network. They determine both travel time and operational costs. It is therefore essential to know what the main relationships for these design variables are, and, given these relationships, what the optimal values are for planning purposes.

The network design problem can always be seen as finding a balance between opposing objectives: in the case of public transport network design, mainly between the objectives of the traveller and those of the operator. Analytical models are especially suited for analysing such dilemmas.

Review of literature on analytical models for urban public transport network design shows a consensus on objectives and decision variables. Usually a single objective is used. The common objective is minimisation of total costs, that is traveller costs and operator costs. In the case of railway networks, infrastructure costs are included too. More recently, the objective of maximising social welfare, defined as the sum of the net user benefit (consumer surplus) and operator's profit (producer surplus), is used more often. Stop spacing, line spacing and headway are the main decision variables. Some studies use the concept of a variable stop spacing along a public transport line. Most studies assume that there is a fixed level of demand. Only in the case of maximising social welfare, a linear relationship between the supply of public transport and the level of demand is used.

A general framework for building analytical models is described by defining building blocks for all parties involved in public transport network design: the traveller, the operator, and the authorities. Special attention is paid to the description of the relationship between supply and demand, using a logit-model, logit-elasticities and travel-time-ratios.

Using these building blocks and the viewpoints of the three parties involved, seven alternative objectives are formulated for finding related optimal network design parameters:

1. Minimising weighted door-to-door travel time;
2. Minimising weighted door-to-door travel time on a fixed budget;
3. Maximising cost efficiency (revenues divided by costs);
4. Maximising profit;
5. Maximising social welfare;
6. Minimising total costs;
7. Maximising patronage.

For each of these objectives a solution technique has been developed following an analytical approach, including numerical techniques, or using enumeration. These solution techniques are applied to two typical cases:
- A bus network is a small city, having average trip lengths of 3 kilometres;
- A tram network in a large city, having trips lengths of 5 kilometres.

The results are compared for a range of performance characteristics, such as travel time and operator costs.

The analyses show that minimising total costs, while assuming that the level of demand is fixed, and maximising social welfare are the best objectives to be used in network design. Minimising travel time and maximising patronage each result in attractive but expensive network structures. Maximising profit, on the other hand, results in profitable but unattractive network structures. No optimum could be found for the objective of maximising cost efficiency. Since the demand for public transport exhibits a limited sensitivity for the quality of public transport service, minimising operational costs will always result in higher cost efficiency. Minimising travel time under a fixed budget proves to be a suitable objective in the case that an optimal budget has been determined, for instance, using the objective of minimising total costs.

Furthermore, the analysis shows that traditional values adopted for stop spacing and line spacing are too small. For bus networks the stop spacing and the line spacing should be doubled to about 700 metres and to 1,000 metres respectively. This allows for higher frequencies, which make public transport more attractive, especially for short trips. For tram networks, the stop spacing should also be doubled up to 800 metres. These values should not be used as rigid numbers but as averages. This allows explicitly for variation to adapt to typical local circumstances. It has been shown that it is possible to allocate stops using these design guidelines in realistic situations.

A sensitivity analysis shows that it is more plausible to find a motivation for even larger values than for smaller values. Allocating stops at locations having higher demand densities, for instance, will result in significantly larger values for stop spacing. Another important finding is that if the demand level drops, it is best to increase the line spacing in order to maintain acceptable frequencies.

Apart from the analysis of objectives, the impact has been determined of distinguishing different target traveller groups, each having different valuations for the parts of a trip. Choosing for a specific target traveller group results in a variation of the optimal design parameter values of plus or minus 15 % at most for the stop spacing and 30 % at most for line spacing, while choosing a different objective leads to doubling the traditional stop spacing. It is therefore concluded that the choice for an objective has a larger impact on the key design variables than the choice for specific customer groups.

Furthermore, an analysis is made of the impact of using bicycles to access the urban public transport system. It is shown that even for a network that is optimised for cycling as an access mode, walking will still be an important access mode too. As a result the increase in access speed will be limited, leading to an increase of stop spacing and line spacing of 37 % and 55 % respectively. Compared to the situation of walking only the average travel times and especially the operational costs are reduced significantly.

From these findings clear recommendations for planning practice emerge. Current network design focuses too much on short trips and on access distance only, while ignoring in-vehicle time, waiting time, and operational costs. As a result, existing urban public transport networks are too expensive. Opting for a balance between traveller costs and operator costs and focussing on longer trip lengths, will result in twice the traditional stop spacing for bus and tram networks, and in twice the traditional line spacing for bus networks. Implementing these changes will lead to a significant reduction of operational costs, while service quality is maintained or improved and thus ridership is maintained or increased. Improving cycling facilities at and around stops will further enhance these favourable shifts.

Contents

1 INTRODUCTION 1

2 CHARACTERISTICS OF THE PUBLIC TRANSPORT NETWORK DESIGN PROBLEM 5
   2.1 Design dilemmas 5
   2.2 Design objectives 10
      2.2.1 Traveller's interests 10
      2.2.2 Operator's interests 10
      2.2.3 Authority's objectives 11
      2.2.4 Summary of objectives 12
   2.3 Design problem for stop spacing and line spacing 13

3 PUBLIC TRANSPORT NETWORK DESIGN PROBLEM IN RETROSPECT 15
   3.1 Design problem of public transport service networks 15
   3.2 Solution techniques 19
   3.3 Characteristics of the results 19
   3.4 Conclusions 20

4 BUILDING BLOCKS FOR NETWORK DESIGN OBJECTIVES 21
   4.1 Problem definition 21
   4.2 Travel time 22
   4.3 Transport demand functions 25
   4.4 Operator's criteria 27
   4.5 Authority's criteria 28

5 OBJECTIVE FUNCTIONS FOR PUBLIC TRANSPORT NETWORK DESIGN 33
   5.1 Traveller oriented objective functions 33
   5.2 Operator oriented objective functions 34

	5.3	Authority oriented objective functions	34
	5.4	Discussion	35
	5.5	Selection of promising objectives	37

6 SOLVING OPTIMISATION MODELS ... 39

	6.1	O1: Minimising weighted travel time	39
	6.2	O2: Minimising weighted travel time on a fixed budget	42
	6.3	O3: Maximising cost efficiency	44
	6.4	O4: Maximising profit	46
	6.5	O5: Maximising social welfare	46
	6.6	O6: Minimising total costs	47
		6.6.1 Assuming a fixed demand level	47
		6.6.2 Using the logit-mode-choice model	48
		6.6.3 Solving for stop spacing, line spacing, and frequency simultaneously	48
	6.7	O7: Maximising patronage	49
	6.8	Conclusions	51

7 NUMERICAL RESULTS ... 53

	7.1	Characteristics of the analysis	53
	7.2	Bus network	55
	7.3	Tram network	58
	7.4	Sensitivity analysis	60
		7.4.1 Sensitivity for O6.2: Minimising total costs	60
		7.4.2 Sensitivity for other objective functions	63
		7.4.3 Sensitivity for the relationship between supply and demand	64
	7.5	Conclusions	65

8 IMPLICATIONS FOR PLANNING PRACTICE ... 67

	8.1	Importance of choosing objectives	67
	8.2	Adopting larger stop and line spacing	70
	8.3	Case studies	72

9 FURTHER ANALYSES USING ANALYTICAL MODELS ... 77

	9.1	Extension to a network	77
		9.1.1 Conceptual approach	78

		9.1.2 Formalisation 79
		9.1.3 Radial network 81
	9.2	Extension to daily operations 84
	9.3	Stop spacing in city centres 86
	9.4	Influence of opting for specific traveller groups 87
	9.5	Impact of a multimodal approach 89
		9.5.1 Cycling instead of walking 89
		9.5.2 Realistic shares for cycling 91
		9.5.3 Impact on demand level 93
		9.5.4 Formal approach 94
		9.5.5 Conclusions 98

10 CONCLUSIONS AND FURTHER RESEARCH 101

    10.1 Theoretical conclusions 101

    10.2 Recommendations for planning practice 103

    10.3 Recommendations for further research 105

References

Appendix A: **Argumentation for using average travel distances**

Appendix B: **Derivation of costs factors for bus and tram**

Appendix C: **Optimisation of variable stop spacing**

List of symbols

Chapter 1

INTRODUCTION

Stop spacing and line spacing are key design variables in urban public transport networks. They determine both the travel times for the travellers and the costs for the operator. Stop spacing influences the average speed of a public transport vehicle. Line spacing determines the frequency of public transport lines and thus the waiting time. Both factors determine the access distance and thus the access time. On their turn the average speed, the number of lines, and the frequency determine the operator's costs. It is therefore essential to know what the main relationships for these design variables are, and what the best or optimal values are for planning practice. These are exactly the questions this report focuses on.

Existing urban public transport service networks have usually developed using a traditional way of planning. Existing values for stop spacing and line spacing have been used in the expansion of public transport networks. Table 1-1 shows actual values for stop spacing values in Dutch cities found in 1998, which are in the range of 350 and 450 metres. It is interesting to notice that the values for stop spacing in tram networks are more or less identical to those for bus networks. Furthermore, there seems to be no correlation with city size. Values found for line spacing are, roughly put, 1.000 metres for tram networks, for instance, in the southern part of The Hague, and 500 metres for bus networks, e.g. the neighbourhoods Zuilen and Overvecht in Utrecht.

In the cases that, instead of traditional design approaches, a network optimisation model has been used, values for stop spacing and line spacing are implicitly assumed by the definition of zones and of the link network which are used in the optimisation model. Examples of such optimisation models can be found in Van Nes et al. (1988), Caramia et al. (1998), Carrese & Gori (1998) and Ceder & Israeli (1999). Again, the existing network structure implicitly determines the design process. Different assumptions for zones and initial link network, and therefore for stop spacing and line spacing, might result in different designs for the public transport network.

Table 1-1: Average stop spacing in metres for a sample of cities in the Netherlands (Author's calculations, 1998)

City	Average stop spacing
Amsterdam (tram)	400
Rotterdam (tram)	425
The Hague (tram)	400
Rotterdam	450
The Hague	425
Utrecht	375
Eindhoven	450
Groningen	350
Arnhem	450
Maastricht	450
Amersfoort	425
Dordrecht	375

Given the historical growth of urban public transport networks, it is not strange that the adoption of what seemed to be good planning practice prevailed in public transport network design. In times that cost efficiency of urban public transport systems is at stake, however, special attention for these common 'facts' is needed. Is prevailing planning practice really good planning practice, or have the underlying principles and assumptions changed over time?

In this report an analysis is made of the main relationships between stop spacing and line spacing on the one hand, and travel times and operator's costs on the other hand. Since analytical models are especially suited for the analysis of design problems having conflicting points of view, these models are used as the main tool in this study. The objective of this study is to derive guidelines for optimal stop and line spacing values given a chosen planning objective to be achieved.

The problem studied in this report is not limited to urban public transport networks only. Combination of stop spacing and line spacing results in the access density, that is, the number of stops per unit area. The concept of access density is universal in transport network design. Examples are the number of on- and off-ramps for a freeway network and the number of distribution centres in a goods distribution network. The methods and analyses presented in this report are therefore suitable for similar network design problems for all kind of transport networks, and vice versa (see for instance Daganzo (1999)).

This report is structured as follows. The main characteristics of the public transport network design problem are discussed in Chapter 2. What are the design dilemmas, which parties are involved, and what are their preferred objectives? Chapter 3 presents an overview of literature on the optimisation of stop spacing and line spacing. The main characteristics of the design problem will be presented as well as different approaches to formulate and to solve the design problem. In Chapter 4 the basic building blocks of an analytical model are described, which are then used in Chapter 5 to define optimisation models for different objectives. These objectives are based on the viewpoints of the traveller, the operator and the authorities respectively. Chapter 6 discusses techniques to solve the optimisation models and discusses some typical characteristics of the design problem. Chapter 7 presents numerical results for a typical bus network and a typical tram network respectively, including a sensitivity analysis. Chapter 8 focuses on the implications for planning practice, such as the importance of choosing an objective, the consequences for urban public transport network design in general and for specific cases. Chapter 9 discusses some further analyses using the models developed in this report, for instance, the extension to a network and to daily operations, the influence of opting for specific traveller groups, and the impact of a multimodal approach in urban public transport systems. Finally, Chapter 10 summarises the main findings, formulates recommendations for planning practice, and suggests subjects for further research.

The use of analytical models implies mathematics. In order to follow the main arguments discussed in this report, however, it is not necessary to go through all the mathematical formulations. Given the extensive discussion of the design problem for urban public transport networks in Chapter 2, it is possible to skip Chapters 3 to 6 and to go straight to Chapter 7 for the numerical results and Chapter 8 for the implications for planing practice. In a similar way it is possible to skip the mathematical parts in Chapter 9.

Chapter 2

CHARACTERISTICS OF THE PUBLIC TRANSPORT NETWORK DESIGN PROBLEM

In this chapter the main characteristics of the public transport network design problem will be discussed. First, attention is given to the dilemmas in network design. This is followed by a discussion on objectives that might be used in network design. The last section focuses especially on the design problem of stop spacing and line spacing.

2.1 Design dilemmas

The main characteristic of network design is the balance between opposing objectives. A design that is optimal with respect to one objective is not optimal for another objective, and vice versa. The main controversy in transport network design is the difference between the traveller and the builder, or operator, as can be shown in Figure 2-1.

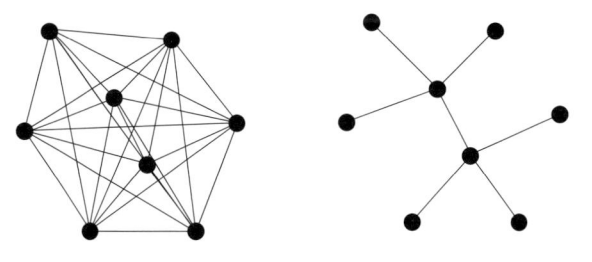

User's optimum   Builder's or operator's optimum

Figure 2-1: Illustration of the user's and the builder's, or operator's, optimum

The builder or operator likes to have the smallest network possible, resulting in a minimum spanning tree, while the user is focused on the shortest travel time, resulting in a fully connected network. Both solutions are optimal from one point of view but are clearly unsuitable from the other point of view.

For public transport networks the design dilemma can be formulated as looking for short travel times versus low operational costs, and since travel time determines patronage, the dilemma can also be formulated as high patronage versus low operational costs.

But even given a specific point of view, for instance that of the traveller, design dilemmas do exist. Egeter (1993) defined four design dilemmas for the design of an urban public transport network, in which he focused on the traveller's point of view given a fixed operational budget:

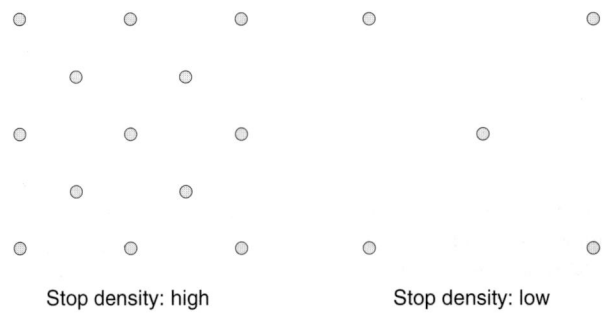

Figure 2-2: Options for the design dilemma of stop densities

1. Short access times versus short in-vehicle times (Figure 2-2). Many stops per square kilometre result in short access distances. On the other hand, the buses have to stop at every stop leading to very low speeds and thus large in-vehicle times.

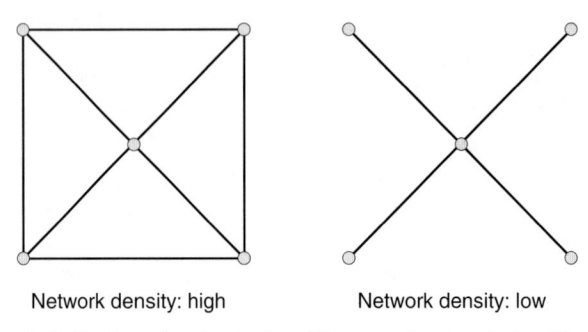

Figure 2-3: Options for the design dilemma of network densities

Chapter 2 Characteristics of the public transport network design problem 7

2. Short in-vehicle times versus short waiting times (Figure 2-3). High network densities, that is the total length of links used by public transport per square kilometre, lead to direct routes and thus short in-vehicles times. On the other hand the number of buses per link will decrease, resulting in low frequencies and long waiting times.

Line density: high   Line density: low

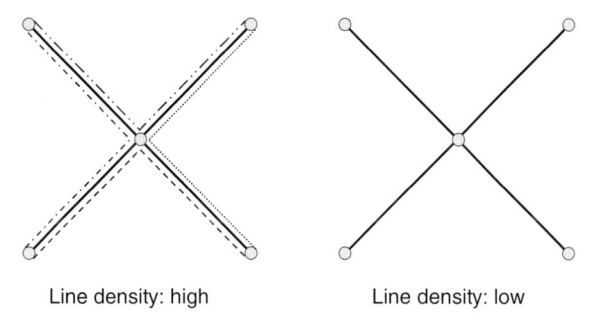

Figure 2-4: Options for the design dilemma of line densities

3. Short waiting times versus minimisation of transfers (Figure 2-4). High line density, that is, total line length per square kilometre, results in a minimum number of transfers, but at the same time to low frequencies per line and thus to large waiting times.

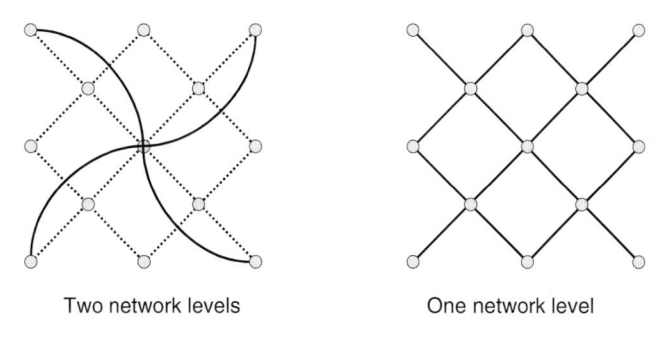

Two network levels   One network level

Figure 2-5: Options for the design dilemma of network levels

4. Minimisation of transfers versus short travel times (Figure 2-5). Distinguishing different network levels results in short travel times as each network will be more suited for specific trip lengths. At the same time, however, different network levels leads to transfers between network levels.

The first three design dilemmas, stop density, network density, and line density, can be applied for each network level distinguished using the fourth design dilemma.

Given the focus of this report, that is assessing optimal relationships for stop and line spacing for urban public transport networks, only the design dilemmas 1, stop density, and 3, line density, are relevant. The dilemmas of network density and line density are strongly correlated. The dilemma of network density has the disadvantage that the line-bound characteristics of pubic transport are not taken into account, while the dilemma of line density implicitly accounts for the network density dilemma too. In many urban public transport networks only single level networks can be found. The design dilemma of different network levels becomes interesting if large urban agglomerations are studied.

The concepts of stop density and line density are still somewhat theoretical. There is, for instance, no explicit relationship between stop density and public transport lines. However, if a specific network structure is assumed, these theoretical concepts can be translated into more understandable design variables such as stop spacing and line spacing. In the case of an urban corridor having parallel lines to and from the city centre these relationships can be illustrated as in Figure 2-6.

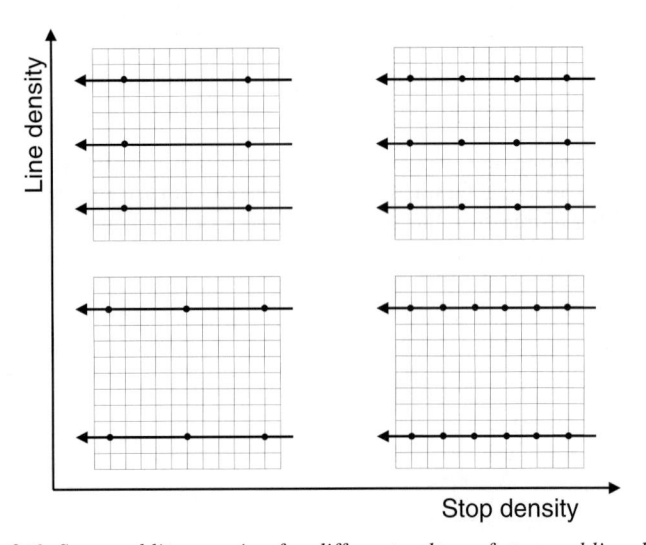

Figure 2-6: Stop and line spacing for different values of stop and line density

In this case, line spacing is equivalent to line density and stop spacing varies as a function of line density and stop density: given a specific stop density the stop spacing increases as line density, or line spacing, increases. Given a fixed operational budget, these networks can be ranked for characteristics such as frequency, access distance, and vehicle speed, see Figure 2-7. The controversy between different characteristics is clear: what is best for frequency is worst access distance, et cetera.

Chapter 2 Characteristics of the public transport network design problem   9

$$\frac{3\ |\ 4}{1\ |\ 2} \qquad \frac{3\ |\ 1}{4\ |\ 2} \qquad \frac{1\ |\ 3}{2\ |\ 4}$$

Frequency   Access   Vehicle
              distance   speed

Figure 2-7: Ranking of networks for frequency, access distance, and vehicle speed (1 is best, 4 is worst)

Another way to look at the design dilemma is shown in Figure 2-8. In this case only stop spacing is considered. Short stop spacing results in low access times, and as stop spacing increases, access time increases too. The in-vehicle time, on the other hand, depends on the number of stops; more stops imply larger in vehicle times or, formulated the other way around, larger stop spacing implies lower in-vehicle times. Adding access time and in-vehicle time yields the travel time as a function of the stop spacing. For simplicity, waiting time and egress time are assumed to be constant. The graph shows that there is a value for the stop spacing for which the travel time is minimal. Of course, this optimal value for the stop spacing can also be found using analytical methods.

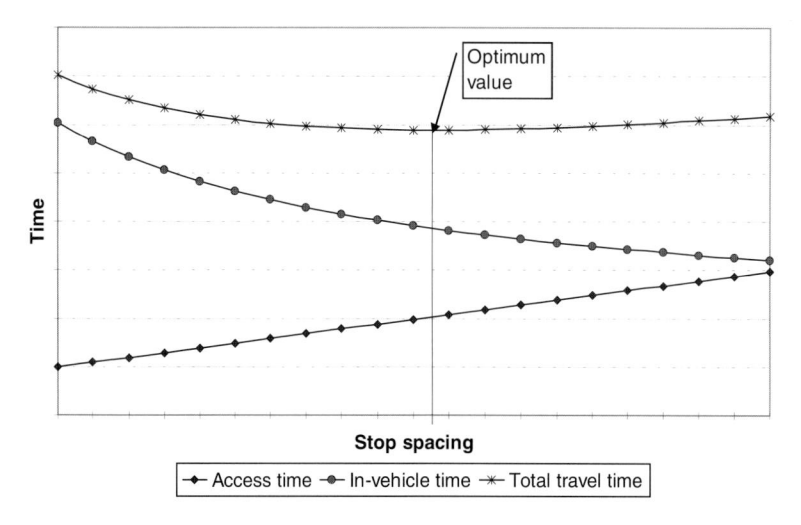

Figure 2-8: Illustration of the design dilemma of access time versus in-vehicle time

This discussion of design dilemmas shows clearly that the main problem in network design is to find a balance between opposing influences. The question is then what the designer tries to achieve, or what kind of objective is being used in network design. The last example on the dilemma between access time and in-vehicle time implies minimisation of the total travel time, but there are clearly other objectives that might be used in public transport network design.

2.2 Design objectives

In public transport network design there are three parties involved, each of them having their own point of view on the objective that has to be used: traveller, operator, and authorities respectively.

2.2.1 Traveller's interests

Travellers judge transport services mainly by three components: travel time, costs, and comfort. The main interest of the traveller is the door-to-door travel time, or more correctly, the perceived door-to-door travel time, which is determined by the public transport network design. A trip by public transport consists of different time elements, having their own weight in the perception of the traveller: access time, waiting time, in-vehicle time, transfer time, and egress time. If network design is focused on the interest of the traveller, a possible objective would be minimising the total weighted travel time. This objective, however, lacks the controversy between traveller and builder or operator. Ultimately, this could lead to fully connected networks, which are clearly unsuitable from the operator's point of view. A more realistic formulation would be minimising total weighted travel time, given a fixed operational budget. The question is then what this budget should be. That is where the viewpoints of the other two parties involved in public transport network design come in.

2.2.2 Operator's interests

The main interests of any company, and thus of a public transport company too, are continuity and profitability. The balance between these interests will vary between companies. The minimum required for continuity is a break-even operation. On the long run, however, profitability is essential to guarantee continuity. Therefore, the viewpoint of the operator might be formulated as maximising profit, that is revenue minus operational costs, or as maximising cost efficiency or maximising revenue per unit of costs, that is revenue divided by operational costs. The subject revenue used in these objectives deserves some further attention. Public transport companies have two types of clients: the traveller and the authorities. The number of travellers and the fare they pay determine the revenues from the traveller, who is sensitive to the quality of the services offered. The revenue from the authorities might be a fixed sum, a subsidy per traveller, or even a subsidy per kilometre travelled.

A possible strategy for an operator, for instance, is to reduce operational costs by reducing service quality. This will lead to less travellers and therefore to less revenues too. The net effect however, might be positive form the operator's point of view. In the case of a subsidy per traveller, this will reduce the total subsidy too. If a lump sum subsidy is relevant, the net effect for the operator will be larger. It is interesting to notice that a strategy to reduce operational costs will have a larger impact on the objective of maximising cost efficiency, since it formulated as the ratio of revenues and operational costs, as on maximising profit.

2.2.3 Authority's objectives

The authorities, the third party involved, have different viewpoints. From a societal point of view the objective might be maximising social benefit, which can be formulated as maximising social welfare or as minimising total costs. Both formulations include benefits for the travellers as well as for the operator. Social welfare is defined as the sum of consumer surplus and operator surplus.

The principle of surplus is the value gained by users and operators by offering a specific service. In the case of an operator the operator surplus can be formulated as operator's profit: the operator would be willing to provide a specific service under break-even conditions and any increase in revenue can be considered as value gained. If the same principle is applied to travellers, the principle of consumer surplus results: travellers who would be willing to travel at higher travel costs and can travel having lower travel cost gain the difference in time and money.

Figure 2-9 presents an illustration of consumer surplus in an economic context. The demand curve shows that given high travel costs only few travellers will actually use the service. If travel costs are reduced, the use of the service increases. However, in order to accommodate the travellers, the travel costs increase, which is shown in the supply curve. In the situation that there is a balance between demand and supply, the consumer surplus or the costs gained by travellers who would be willing to travel at higher travel costs can be shown by the grey area.

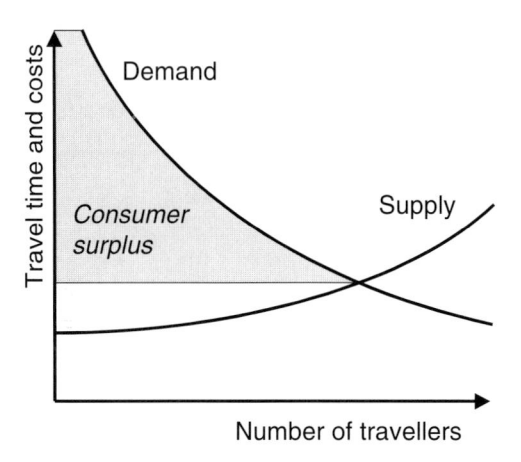

Figure 2-9: The concept of consumer surplus

Minimisation of total costs is an alternative for maximising social welfare. Total costs are defined as the sum of all costs involved in travelling and all operational costs. The costs involved in travelling includes travel times and fares. Travel times are transformed into costs using value-of-time factors. However, since fares paid by the travellers reduce the costs for the operator, they can be excluded from the total costs, which then consists of all travel times and operational costs.

A second viewpoint of the authorities is offered by transportation policy. In order to reduce the negative impacts of travelling by private car, a possible objective might be to maximise patronage. Since travel time is the main characteristic for travellers, this objective is more or less equivalent to minimising travel time.

The third viewpoint of the authorities is financial one: minimising the amount of subsidy. This objective is, in a certain way, equivalent to the operator's objective of maximising profit.

Apart from defining design objectives, authorities might play another role in public transport network design, namely setting constraints, such as a maximum access distance or a minimum frequency. In this case, the operator can use his own objective in public transport network design as long as these constraints are fulfilled. Of course, the resulting network will be less optimal as the operator would have liked it to be. The key question is which constraints should be used. The use of the objectives formulated from the authority's point of view might answer this question.

2.2.4 Summary of objectives

The discussion in this section presented seven objectives for public transport network design:

1. Minimising perceived door-to-door travel time;
2. Minimising perceived door-to-door travel time on a fixed budget;
3. Maximising cost efficiency (revenues divided by costs);
4. Maximising profit (or minimising subsidy);
5. Maximising social welfare;
6. Minimising total costs;
7. Maximising patronage.

Given these objectives the following remarks can be made:
- Since the objective of minimising travel time only does not account for operational costs, this objective might be considered to be rather naïve.
- Since maximising cost efficiency is defined by the ratio of revenues and operational costs is might sensitive for changes in operational costs. The objective of maximising profits might therefor be more robust.
- Since the demand for public transport strongly depends on the perceived door-to-door travel time the objective of maximising patronage might be equivalent to the objective minimising travel time only.

2.3 Design problem for stop spacing and line spacing

This report focuses on assessing optimal relationships for the key design variables stop spacing and line spacing. Figure 2-10 shows the main relationships for these design variables with respect to the network design objectives formulated in the previous Section.

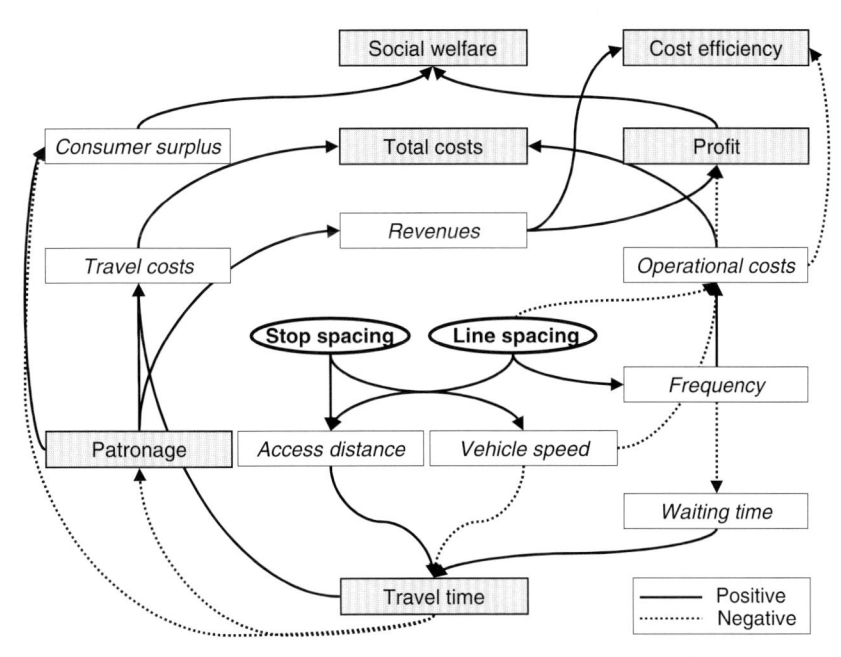

Figure 2-10: Relationships of stop spacing and line spacing on network design objectives

An increase in stop spacing, for instance, results in an increase of the access distance, and thus access time, and finally in an increase of travel time. At the same time, the increase of stop spacing leads to higher vehicle speeds, leading to a reduction of travel time. A similar line of reasoning can be applied to an increase of the line spacing. This too results in an increase of the access distance and therefore the travel time. However, the increase of stop spacing also allows for an increase of the frequency, leading to a reduction of waiting time and therefore of travel time. The net effect on travel time depends on the way travel time is defined, and on the values of the parameters used. The relationships for all other objectives can be identified in an identical manner.

In the following chapters an analytical approach is used to determine optimal relationships for the design variables stop spacing and line spacing for each objective. First, the mathematical descriptions of these relationships will be presented. These relationships will then be used as building blocks to define objective functions, which are mathematical representations of the formulated objectives. Optimising these objective functions with respect to the decision variables stop spacing and line spacing yields the optimal relationships for these decision variables using the various design parameters and system parameters, and the performance of the specific objective function. The optimal relationships can finally be used to calculate the characteristics for other criteria to judge a public transport network design.

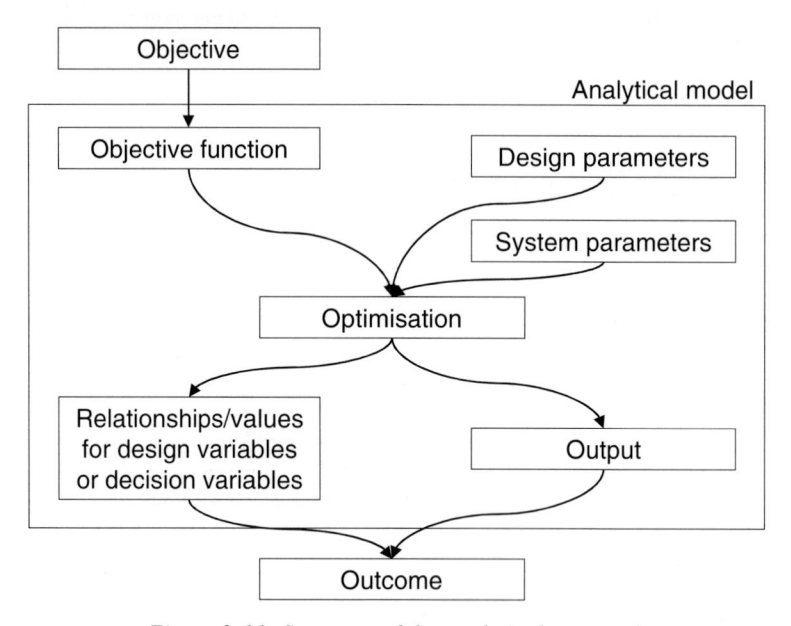

Figure 2-11: Structure of the analytical approach

In this approach the following terminology is used (Figure 2-11):

- Objective: the criterion or set of criteria to be optimised, for instance, maximising patronage;
- Objective function: mathematical formulation of the objective;
- Design variables or decision variables: endogenous variables for which optimal relationships or optimal values have to be determined, in this case the design variables are stop spacing and line spacing;
- Design parameters: exogenously given parameters used in the mathematical formulation that are not determined by the public transport system itself, for instance, the weights for the various time elements;
- System parameter: exogenously given parameters used in the mathematical formulation that are determined by the public transport system itself, for instance, the costs of operating a bus;
- Output: results of the analytical model, for instance, the value of the objective function;
- Outcome: the total set of criteria used to judge a network design, such as travel time, perceived travel time, operational costs, et cetera.

Chapter 3

PUBLIC TRANSPORT NETWORK DESIGN PROBLEM IN RETROSPECT

Before formulating analytical models for the objectives discussed in Chapter 2, a review of such analytical models found in literature will be presented. This discussion includes the following subjects:

- Problem description;
- Solution techniques;
- Characteristics of the results.

Finally, section 3.4 will present the conclusions from this analysis.

3.1 Design problem of public transport service networks

The general structure of the problem description for an analytical model is:

- Set of decision variables;
- Objective function, mathematical formulation of the objective using the decision variables;
- Optionally a set of constraints with respect to the decision variables or to intermediate variables.

There is a considerable amount of studies on analytical models for public transport network design, as can be seen in the overview presented in Table 3-1.

Table 3-1: Historical overview of analytical models in literature

	Network	Demand	Decision variables	Objectives	Constraints
Holroyd (1967)	Grid	Many-to-many	Line spacing Headway	Travel costs + operating costs	
Black (1978)	Radial	Many-to-one	Stop spacing Line spacing Headway Route length	Travel costs + operating costs + investments costs + fleet costs	
Newell (1979)	Grid	Many-to-many	Line spacing Headway	Travel costs + operating costs	
Brändli et al. (1980)	Urban corridor	Many-to-one	Stop spacing	Travel time	
Wirasinghe (1980)	Feeder	Many-to-one	Stop spacing Line spacing Headway	Travel costs + operating costs	
Wirasinghe & Gnoheim (1981)	Single route	Many-to-many	Stop spacing Line spacing	Travel costs + operating costs	
Kocur & Hendrickson (1982)	Urban corridor	Many-to-one	Line spacing Headway Fare	Profit Consumer surplus + profit Consumer surplus only	Vehicle capacity Operating budget
Tsao & Schonfeld (1983)	Zone stop schedule	Many-to-one	Headway Number of zones	Travel costs + operating costs	Vehicle capacity
Tsao & Schonfeld (1984)	Zone stop schedule	Many-to-one	Headway Number of zones	Travel costs + operating costs	Vehicle capacity
Wirasinghe & Seneviratne (1986)	Urban corridor	Many-to-one	Route length	Travel costs + operating costs + investment costs + fleet costs	
Gnoheim & Wirasinghe (1987)	Zone stop schedule	Many-to-one	Stop spacing Headway Route length	Travel costs + operating costs + fleet costs + station costs	

Chapter 3 Public transport network design problem in retrospect

	Network	Demand	Decision variables	Objectives	Constraints
Kuah & Perl (1988)	Feeder	Many-to-one	Stop spacing Line spacing Headway	Travel costs + operating costs	
Chang & Schonfeld (1991)	Zone stop schedule + DRT	Many-to-one	Line spacing Vehicle size	Travel costs + operating costs	
Chang & Schonfeld (1993a)	Zone stop schedule	Many-to-one	Line spacing Headway Route length	Travel costs + operating costs	
Spasovic & Schonfeld (1993)	Urban corridor	Many-to-one	Stop spacing Line spacing Headway Route length	Travel costs + operating costs	
Chang & Schonfeld (1993b)	Zone stop schedule	Many-to-one	Stop spacing Line spacing Headway Route length	Social welfare	Subsidy
Egeter (1993/1995)	Urban corridor	Many-to-one	Stop spacing Line spacing Headway	Travel time	Operation budget
Spasovic et al. (1994)	Urban corridor	Many-to-one	Line spacing Headway Route length Fare	Profit Social welfare	Subsidy Vehicle capacity
Chang & Yu (1996)	Zone stop schedule + DRT	Many-to-one	Headway Zone size Fare	Social welfare	Subsidy
Liu et al. (1996)	Single route	Many-to-many	Route length	Travel costs + operating costs + investment costs + fleet costs	

DRT = Demand responsive transit, usually flexible routes

The early models are concerned with simplified public transport networks. Most studies, however, focus on specific network types, such as corridors or even on single routes. For studies concerning a corridor a distinction can be made in traditional public transport lines, feeder lines, and zone stop schedules. In the latter case a line can be divided in two parts: an express route to and from the city centre, and a route for collecting and distributing passengers within a zone.

The demand pattern that is assumed in the analyses is usually a many-to-one pattern, mainly trips to the city centre or a railway line. Many-to-many patterns are analysed for grid networks and for single routes.

Commonly used decision variables are:
- Stop spacing, the distance between subsequent stops of a line;
- Line spacing, the distance between parallel lines;
- Headway, the distance in time between subsequent vehicles on a line;
- Route length.

In some studies the decision variables are replaced by functions, which allow the optimal values to vary along the route, see for instance Wirasinghe (1980), Wirasinghe & Gnoheim (1981), Wirasinghe & Seneviratne (1986) and Kuah & Perl (1988).

The main objective used in literature is minimising total costs, either the sum of travel costs and operating costs, or the sum of travel costs, operating costs and capital costs, that is investment costs and fleet costs. Investment costs are usually introduced in the analysis of railway systems. Recently the more sophisticated and more complex objective of maximising social welfare, defined as the sum of consumer surplus and producer surplus, is used too. The use of the concept of consumer surplus requires that the level of demand depends on the quality offered. In these models a simplified linear relationship is used. In all other analytical models the demand level is fixed. An exception in the objectives found in literature is the one used by Egeter (1993): minimising total travel time.

The use of constraints in analytical models is limited (see Table 3-1). The operating budget is relevant in the case of objectives focused on the traveller's point of view only. Subsidy is used to achieve an acceptable service level. The question is what the level of subsidy should be. An interesting constraint is vehicle capacity. The common way is to define a relationship between demand, headway and vehicle capacity or the average vehicle occupancy. It might be questioned, however, whether this constraint is not too detailed, compared with all other assumption made in the models.

In two studies (Chang & Schonfeld (1991), Chang & Yu (1996)) attention is paid to the possibility of introducing flexible routes for distributing and collecting passengers within a zone.

Limited attention is given to the choice of the objective, and the influence of this choice on the final outcome. The only exception is the study by Kocur & Hendrickson (1982). Furthermore, most studies are concerned with a single network structure only. No comparison is made between different optimal network structures. Finally, only single level networks are considered. Only the work of Egeter (1993, 1995) considers multi-level public transport networks.

Chapter 3 Public transport network design problem in retrospect 19

3.2 Solution techniques

Basically, there are two solution techniques: the analytical approach and enumeration. The advantage of the analytical approach is that for each decision variable the optimal relationships with the parameters and other decision variables are defined explicitly. Such relationships clearly show which variables and which parameters are most important for an optimal public transport network. The disadvantage is that the design problem must be formulated in such a way that the objective function is suitable for mathematical analysis. Enumeration allows for mathematically less tractable formulations of the objective, but provides less clear insight into the main relationships for the decision variables.

The analytical approach is used most often. Only Egeter (1993) uses enumeration. In the analytical approach the design problem is solved by differentiating the objective function with respect to the decision variables. In the case that constraints are used, such as the operating budget or the subsidy level, the constraints are usually included into the objective using Lagrange multipliers. The resulting set of equations is either solved analytically or, in the case of more complicated equations, solved numerically, for instance using Gauss-Seidel iteration schemes.

3.3 Characteristics of the results

The main characteristics found in nearly all studies is that the optimal relationships for the decision variables can be described using square root or cubic root functions. This finding implies that the optimal values have a limited sensitivity with respect to the parameters and variables used. Doubling the value of a design parameter, or of a system parameter, results in an increase of the decision variable of 41 % (square root relationship) or 26 % (cubic root) at most, or in the case of an inverse relationship, a maximum decrease of 29 % (square root) or 21 % (cubic root).

The objective functions are shallow around the optimum (see also Figure 2-8). This result allows for varying the values in planning practice, for instance in order to account for typical characteristics of an urban area, without serious consequences for the design objective. However, it is important to notice that due to the square root and cubic root relationships, lower values for the decision variables will have more impact on the value of the objective function than higher values.

A common finding is that at the optimum the travel time components that depend on the decision variables should be equal, for instance, access time should equal time lost at stops. This finding has been reported by e.g. Holroyd (1967), Kocur & Hendrickson (1982), Tsao & Schonfeld (1983), and Spasovic & Schonfeld (1993) respectively.

Two other typical findings that might be relevant for planning practice are:

- In the case that stop spacing is allowed to vary along the route and that a many-to-one demand pattern is assumed, stop spacing increases towards the destination. The introduction of extra stops close to the destination results in significant time losses for the passengers that are already on the line;
- The studies that also accounted for more demand responsive types of public transport all concluded that traditional public transport is more efficient with regard to the objectives used.

3.4 Conclusions

This overview shows a clear pattern with respect to the decision variables and objectives used in the problem definition. Logically, most studies focus on typical situations and use a single objective. The choice of objective is seldom discussed. Welfare maximisation seems to be the preferable objective, while minimising total costs might be easier to analyse. It is especially this topic, the impact of the choice for specific objectives, that this report focuses on.

A distinction can be made between two types of decision variables: average values or density functions that vary along the routes. The disadvantages of density functions are that they are strongly dependent on the boarding and alighting pattern along the route thus requiring detailed data, and the fact that it is questionable to consider all possible trips in the analysis. Focussing on specific trip types, for instance, trips to the city centre only, might be better to insure high quality for the primary functions of public transport lines. In this report, therefore, only average values are considered. An example of an approach based on density functions can be found in Appendix C.

Most studies assume a fixed demand level for public transport. In the case of welfare maximization a linear relationship is assumed between demand for public transport and the service level of the public transport system. In this study special attention will be given to the consequences of using a more complete description of this relationship, for instance, a logit mode-choice model.

The concept of zone-stop schedules is found quite often in literature, but is not a regular concept in the Netherlands. This concept implies a kind of hierarchical system in which each line serves a subsequent zone or put otherwise serves a specific class of travel distances. It might be interesting to analyse whether this concept might be suitable for the Netherlands. Hierarchical networks, however, are not the subject of this report.

Chapter 4

BUILDING BLOCKS FOR NETWORK DESIGN OBJECTIVES

This chapter discusses mathematical descriptions of the building blocks needed to develop analytical models for an urban corridor. These building blocks are equivalent to the relationships shown in Figure 2-10. First the situation for which the design problem is formulated is presented. Given this problem definition the building blocks for travel time, for travel demand, for the operator, and for the authorities are presented. These building blocks, which are identified using the label BBx, are used in the next chapter to develop objective functions.

4.1 Problem definition

A public transport network can often be simplified into a set of urban corridors in which a set of parallel lines offer public transport to and from the city centre. In formulating the building blocks, a unit area is used that is part of that corridor that covers one square kilometre (see also Figure 4-1).

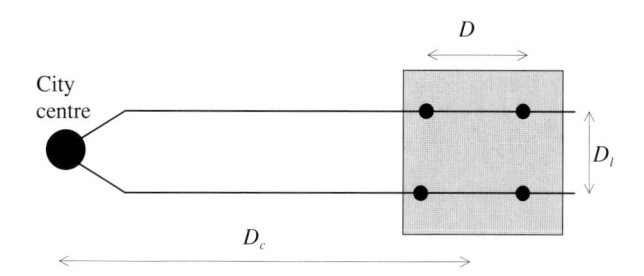

Figure 4-1: Study area and layout of the public transport lines

The demand for public transport is distributed uniformly within this unit area. One or more linear public transport lines serve this area, each having a constant stop spacing D_s. The routes run parallel having a line spacing D_l, and offer public transport to and from the city centre over a given distance D_c. Since the stop spacing D_s and the line spacing D_l are the decision variables, all building blocks will be formulated as functions of these variables.

An important consequence of the focus on network design, and therefore on the key design variables stop spacing and line spacing, is that other system variables, such as frequency or fares, are either assumed to be fixed or are dependent on these key design variables. Fare, for instance, is therefore considered as a system parameter only.

4.2 Travel time

Regarding the traveller, the main characteristic of a public transport network is his total perceived door-to-door travel time. For a trip to the city centre the travel time can be divided into access time, waiting time, in-vehicle time, transfer time, and egress time. Weights are used to account for the fact that travellers have different valuations for the different parts of a trip.

$$\text{BB1:} \quad T_c = w_a \cdot T_a + w_w \cdot T_w + T_i + w_e \cdot T_e \qquad (4\text{-}1)$$

where:
- T_c = total weighted travel time
- T_a = access time
- T_w = waiting time
- T_i = in-vehicle time
- T_e = egress time
- w_x = weight for time element x

Access time T_a, that is the travel time between the origin of the trip and the first stop, depends on the shape of the service area per stop, the routing pattern within the unit area, and the distribution of the demand (see also Figure 4-2).

In the case of rectangular service areas, of access routes parallel and perpendicular to the lines, and of a uniformly distributed demand pattern, the access time can be defined as:

$$\text{BB2:} \quad T_a = \frac{f_a \cdot (D_s + D_l)}{v_a} \qquad (4\text{-}2)$$

where:
- f_a = routing factor for the actual access distance
- v_a = access speed

Chapter 4 Building blocks for design objectives 23

Rectangular service area   Hexagonal service area

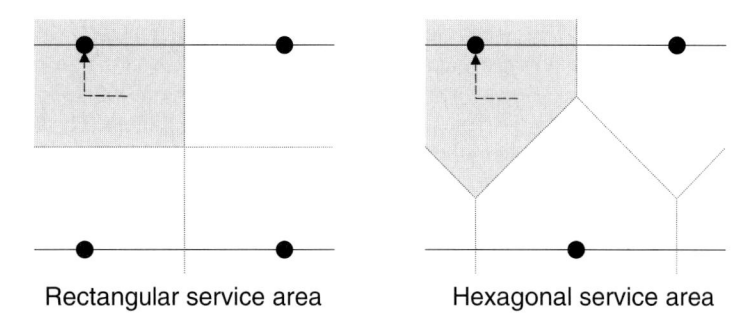

Figure 4-2: Examples of the service area per stop

In this case, the routing factor f_a will equal 0.25. Concentration of the demand around the stops leads to lower values for f_a, just as a radial routing pattern. In the case of hexagonal service areas there will be different routing factors for the parts parallel and perpendicular to the lines. The resulting average routing factor f_a will vary between 0.25 ($D_s=0.5 \cdot D_l$) and 0.22 ($D_s=2 \cdot D_l$) (see Figure 4-3). In this report, however, only rectangular service areas will be considered.

$D_s = 0.5 \cdot D_l$: $f_a=0.247$ $D_s = 2 \cdot D_l$: $f_a=0.222$

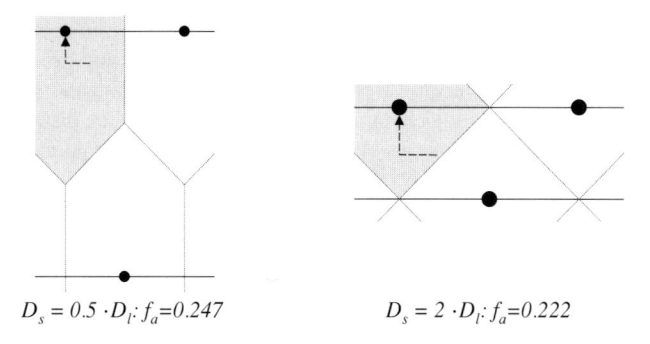

Figure 4-3: Routing factors for typical hexagonal service areas

The traveller's in-vehicle time T_i is determined by the average trip length, the maximum speed and the time lost at each stop due to decelerating, alighting, boarding and accelerating:

$$\text{BB3: } T_i = \frac{D_c}{v} + \frac{D_c}{D_s} \cdot T_s = \frac{D_c}{D_s} \cdot \left(\frac{D_s}{v} + T_s \right) \qquad (4\text{-}3)$$

where:
  v = maximum speed
  T_s = time lost at stops

The choice to use the average trip length D_c is discussed in Appendix A.

From a theoretical point of view, T_s depends on the decision variables D_s and D_l too. Fewer stops might result in a larger number of passengers per stop, and therefore in larger time losses. In this analysis, however, it is assumed that changes in values of decision variables will not significantly influence the boarding and alighting times. Furthermore, it is possible to change boarding and alighting capacity in order to meet a maximum value for the time lost at stops, if necessary.

The waiting time of the traveller depends on the frequency of the services. The frequency can be assumed to be fixed or to depend on the available operational budget B_o. A common definition for the waiting time is half the headway. In this case it is assumed that traveller's arrivals at the stops are uniformly distributed. The waiting time can then be defined as:

$$\text{BB4:} \quad T_w = \frac{f_w}{F} \tag{4-4}$$

where:
   f_w = factor for the waiting time
   F = frequency of the public transport service

Given a fixed operational budget, the frequency is determined by the operational costs per vehicle per period of time (c_o), the number of lines within the unit area (determined by D_l), the travel time within the unit area (determined by D_s), and the fact that the line operates in two directions. This yields the following equation (since distances are defined in metres, the factor 1000 appears to account for the unit area of a square kilometre):

$$\text{BB5:} \quad F = \frac{\frac{B_o}{c_o}}{\frac{1000}{D_l} \cdot \frac{1000}{D_s} \cdot \left(\frac{D_s}{v} + T_s\right) \cdot 2} \tag{4-5}$$

where:
   B_o = available operational budget
   c_o = operational costs per vehicle per hour

Since the focus is on trips to the city centre, it may be assumed that all trips can be made without transfers and that the egress time T_e is fixed.

Substitution of the Equations (4-2) to (4-4) into Equation (4-1) yields the following formulation of the weighted door-to-door travel time to the city centre:

$$T_c = w_a \cdot \frac{f_a \cdot (D_s + D_l)}{v_a} + w_w \cdot \frac{f_w}{F} + \frac{D_c}{D_s} \cdot \left(\frac{D_s}{v} + T_s\right) + w_e \cdot T_e \tag{4-6}$$

4.3 Transport demand functions

Travellers are sensitive for the quality of the services offered. High quality results in high patronage and vice versa. Higher patronage might be due to changes in destination choice or in mode choice. Since public transport has a limited share in modal choice, it is assumed that changes in public transport service quality have limited influence on destination choice. Changes in patronage are then mostly due to changes in mode choice.

From a theoretical point of view, mode choice in influenced by three components: weighted door-to-door travel time, travel costs, and travel comfort. Since the focus is on the design variables stop spacing and line spacing, it is assumed that there will be no differences between alternatives with respect to fares or comfort. As a result, the description of the relationship between supply and demand will be limited tot weighted travel time only.

The relationship for mode choice as a function of travel time can be described using several approaches, for instance:

- Logit-mode-choice;
- Logit-elasticity;
- Travel-time-ratio.

The approach often used in literature is the logit-mode-choice function:

$$\text{BB6:}\quad P(T_c) = P_0 \cdot \frac{\exp(-\alpha \cdot T_c)}{\exp(-\alpha \cdot T_c) + \sum_{m=1}^{n} \exp(-\alpha_m \cdot T_m)} \tag{4-7}$$

where:
- P_0 = total demand for transport per square kilometer in trips
- α = coefficient for public transport
- n = number of modes excluding public transport
- α_m = coefficient for mode m
- T_m = weigthed travel time for mode m

Figure 4-4 shows the share of public transport, that is $P(T_c)/P_0$, as a function of the weighted travel time using a logit-mode-choice model. The dashed line shows the simplification to a linear relationship that is used by for instance Kocur & Hendrickson (1982), Chang & Schonfeld (1993b), Spasovic et al. (1994), and Chang & Yu (1996).

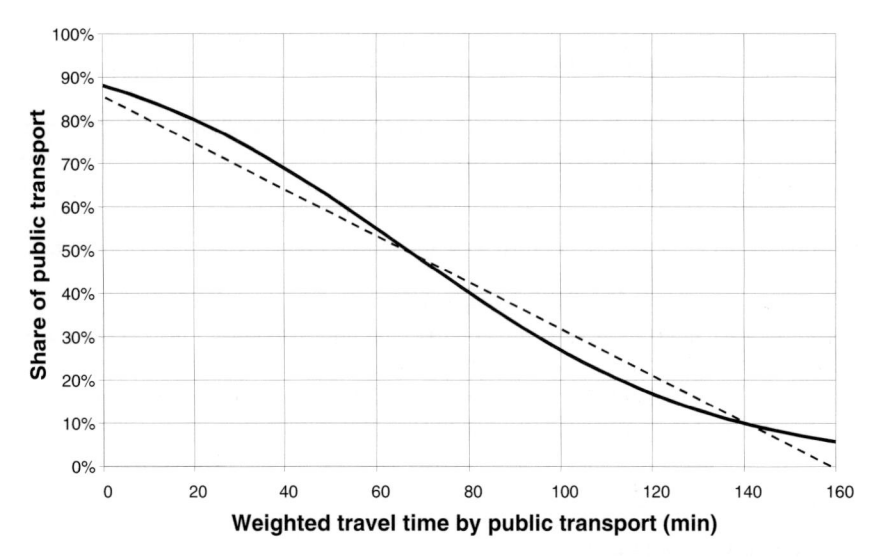

Figure 4-4: Share of public transport as function of the weighted travel time using a logit-mode-choice model

In the case that the share of public transport in mode choice is small, that is, the denominator is large, changes in public transport service quality will not significantly change the value of the denominator. Therefore, the following formulation for the point elasticity for Equation (4-7) can be used:

$$P(T_c) = P_p \cdot \frac{\exp(-\alpha \cdot T_c)}{\exp(-\alpha \cdot \hat{T}_c)} \qquad (4\text{-}8)$$

where:

P_p = demand for public transport in reference situation in trips

$\hat{T}_c$ = weighted travel time for public transport in reference situation

An approach for determining the demand level that is used in the Netherlands (Van Goeverden & Van den Heuvel (1993)) is the travel-time-ratio. This relationship can be formulated as:

$$P = P_0 \cdot \left(\exp\left(\beta \cdot \frac{T_a + T_w + T_i + T_e}{T_p} \right) + \gamma \right) \qquad (4\text{-}9)$$

where:

T_p = travel time by private car

β = coefficient

γ = constant

Since the logit-mode-choice model is used most often, this description will be used throughout this report. The other two descriptions are used for reasons of comparison.

4.4 Operator's criteria

From the point of view of the operator, the main characteristics of the public transport system are its operational costs and revenues.

The operational costs C_o in terms of costs per unit area served are determined by total travel time of the vehicles within the unit area. This travel time depends on the frequency, the number of lines per unit area, the travel time of one vehicle within the unit area, and the fact that the line operates in two directions:

$$\text{BB7: } C_o = c_o \cdot F \cdot \frac{1000}{D_l} \cdot \frac{1000}{D_s} \cdot \left(\frac{D_s}{v} + T_s \right) \cdot 2 \tag{4-10}$$

The revenues for the operator R_o can be defined as:

$$\text{BB8: } R_o = (r_t + r_s) \cdot P \text{ or } R_o = r_t \cdot P + R_s \tag{4-11}$$

where:
- r_t = fare paid by the traveller
- r_s = subsidy paid by the authorities per traveller
- P = number of passengers
- R_s = subsidy paid by the authorities

Fare or subsidy per traveller might be a fixed amount per traveller, as for instance in a zonal fare system, or might be distance related, that is an amount per kilometre travelled. In the latter case Equation (4-11) becomes:

$$R_o = (r_{tk} + r_{sk}) \cdot D_c \cdot P \tag{4-12}$$

where:
- r_{tk} = fare paid by the traveller per kilometre
- r_{sk} = subsidy paid by the authorities per traveller per kilometre

4.5 Authority's criteria

The third party involved in public transport network design is the local authority. From their point of view four building blocks can be defined:

- consumer surplus
- producer surplus or profit
- total travel costs
- operational costs

The operational costs are already defined as building block BB7. The producer surplus or profit can be formulated as revenues minus operational costs, using building blocks BB7 and BB8. In this section, therefore, attention is paid to consumer surplus and total travel costs only.

The concept of consumer surplus has been discussed in Section 2.2.3. It represents the benefits of travellers who can make their trip with lower costs or shorter travel times compared to their maximum acceptable travel costs or travel time. If the logit-mode-choice model as presented in Section 4.3 is used to describe the relationship between supply and demand, the consumer surplus for a given travel time is defined by the grey coloured area in Figure 4-5.

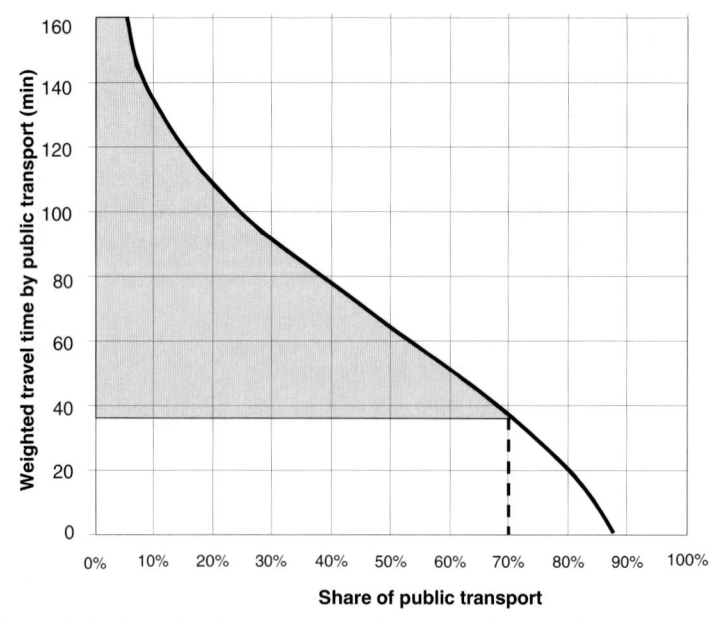

Figure 4-5: Example of consumer surplus using a logit-mode-choice model

Chapter 4 Building blocks for design objectives 29

Due to economic conventions the axes have been switched in comparison with the graph for the logit-mode-choice model as depicted in Figure 4-4. Since the relationship between supply and demand according to building block BB6 is determined by travel time only, the vertical axis represents travel time. In order to monetise travel time, it should be multiplied by the average value of time. Theoretically, fares should be included too in the definition of consumer surplus. However, since fares are assumed to be constant they are dropped in these analyses.

The formula for the consumer surplus S_c for a given door-tot-door travel time T_c becomes:

$$S_c(T_c) = \int_{T_c}^{\infty} P(T_x) dT_x \cdot c_t \qquad (4\text{-}13)$$

where:
c_t = value of time for travelers

The formulation for the consumer surplus using the demand models defined in the following section, however, is rather complicated. A common approximation is to adopt a linear relationship for the demand. The consumer surplus is then calculated as the surface of the grey triangle in Figure 4-6:

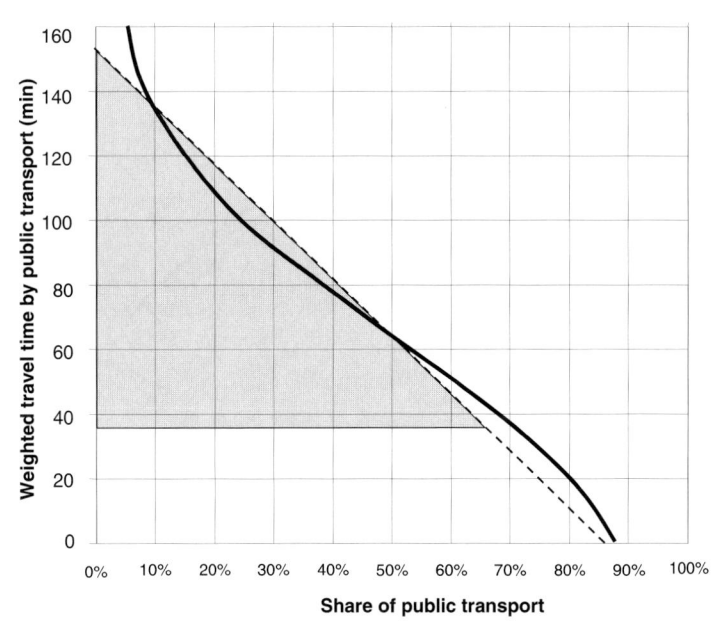

Figure 4-6: Consumer surplus given a linear relationship between supply and demand

Mathematically, this approach results in:

$$S_c(T_c) = 0.5 \cdot P_l(T_c) \cdot (T_{cm} - T_c) \cdot c_t \qquad (4\text{-}14)$$

where:
- P_l = linear relationship for the demand for public transport based on travel time
- T_{cm} = travel time where the demand for public transport vanishes

In this approach the non-linear characteristics of the relationship between travel time and demand are ignored. A compromise between both alternatives might be to assume a triangular shape for the consumer surplus but using the demand level according to the logit-mode-choice model. The maximum travel time T_{cm} can then be calculated, for instance, as the travel time where the share of public transport is no longer sensitive for changes in travel time, e.g. 10 %, or as the weighted travel time for walking only (see Figure 4-7).

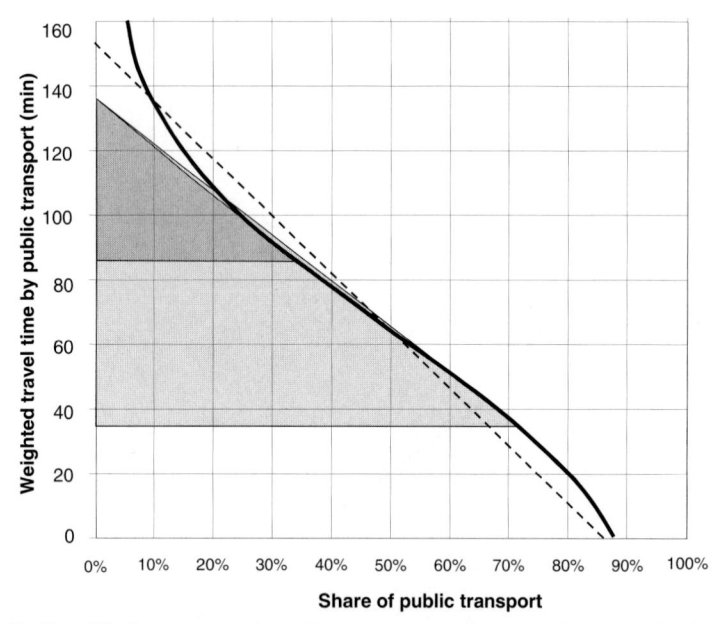

Figure 4-7: Simplified representation of consumer surplus using logit-mode-choice model

In this case the linear description for the demand for public transport in Equation (4-14), that is P_l, is replaced by the logit-mode-choice model. The formula then becomes:

$$\text{BB9: } S_c(T_c) = 0.5 \cdot P(T_c) \cdot (T_{cm} - T_c) \cdot c_t \qquad (4\text{-}15)$$

Since in the analyses in this report the last formulation for the consumer surplus will be used, it is denoted as building block BB9.

Chapter 4 Building blocks for design objectives   31

The last building block to be defined is the total costs for travelling C, which consists of two parts: the total costs for the traveller C_t and the costs for the operator C_o. The total costs for the traveller is defined as:

$$\text{BB10:}\quad C_t = c_t \cdot T_c \cdot P + r_t \cdot P \tag{4-16}$$

where:
$\quad c_t \quad$ = value of time for travelers

Since the fares paid by the traveller reduce the costs for the operator, they can be excluded from the total costs C for travelling, which then becomes:

$$\text{BB11:}\quad C = c_t \cdot T_c \cdot P + C_o \tag{4-17}$$

Chapter 5

OBJECTIVE FUNCTIONS FOR PUBLIC TRANSPORT NETWORK DESIGN

This chapter formulates the various objective functions that can be used in the design of a public transport network with regard to the key design variables stop spacing and line spacing, using the building blocks defined in Chapter 4. The objective functions for the network design problem are presented following the discussion in Chapter 2 on the interests of the three parties involved: traveller, operator, and authorities.

5.1 Traveller oriented objective functions

The main objective of the traveller is minimising his perceived door-to-door travel time. From this point of view, two alternative objective functions are distinguished.

The first objective, that is O1, is minimising weighted travel time in the case that the frequency is fixed. The design problem is then to find a balance between access time and in-vehicle time. Since in this case line spacing only influences access time, the prime decision variable is stop spacing. Line spacing is only relevant if it is assumed that there is a fixed relationship between stop spacing and line spacing, e.g. $D_s = D_l$.

$$\text{O1:} \quad MIN\left\{ w_a \cdot \frac{f_a \cdot (D_s + D_l)}{v_a} + w_w \cdot \frac{f_w}{F} + \frac{D_c}{D_s} \cdot \left(\frac{D_s}{v} + T_s\right) + w_e \cdot T_e \right\} \quad (5\text{-}1)$$

O2 is the second objective: minimising weighted travel time given a fixed operational budget. The introduction of the fixed budget as a constraint allows optimising for both decision variables: stop spacing and line spacing.

$$\text{O2: MIN} \left\{ w_a \cdot \frac{f_a \cdot (D_s + D_l)}{v_a} + w_w \cdot \frac{f_w \cdot \frac{1000}{D_l} \cdot \frac{1000}{D_s} \cdot \left(\frac{D_s}{v} + T_s\right) \cdot 2}{\frac{B_o}{c_o}} + \frac{D_c}{D_s} \cdot \left(\frac{D_s}{v} + T_s\right) + w_e \cdot T_e \right\} \quad (5\text{-}2)$$

The first objective is clearly naive: the interests of the operator have no influence at all in the network design. The second objective is therefore more realistic.

5.2 Operator oriented objective functions

Two objectives have been defined for the operator. The first objective function is maximising the cost effectiveness (O3), defined as the ratio of the total revenues (BB8) and the operational costs (BB7), which is equivalent to maximising ridership per unit cost.

$$\text{O3: MAX} \left\{ \frac{(r_t + r_s) \cdot P_0 \cdot \frac{\exp(-\alpha \cdot T_c)}{\exp(-\alpha \cdot T_c) + \sum_{m=1}^{n} \exp(-\alpha_m \cdot T_m)}}{c_o \cdot F \cdot \frac{1000}{D_l} \cdot \frac{1000}{D_s} \cdot \left(\frac{D_s}{v} + T_s\right) \cdot 2} \right\} \quad (5\text{-}3)$$

The second objective function for the operator is profit maximisation (O4), that is, total revenues reduced by operational costs.

$$\text{O4: MAX} \left\{ (r_t + r_s) \cdot P_0 \cdot \frac{\exp(-\alpha \cdot T_c)}{\exp(-\alpha \cdot T_c) + \sum_{m=1}^{n} \exp(-\alpha_m \cdot T_m)} - c_o \cdot F \cdot \frac{1000}{D_l} \cdot \frac{1000}{D_s} \cdot \left(\frac{D_s}{v} + T_s\right) \cdot 2 \right\} \quad (5\text{-}4)$$

5.3 Authority oriented objective functions

The viewpoint of the authorities resulted in three objectives: maximising social welfare, minimising total costs, and maximising patronage.

Maximising social welfare (O5) can be written as:

Chapter 5 Objective functions for public transport network design

$$O5:\ MAX\left\{(r_t+r_s)\cdot P_0 \cdot \dfrac{\exp(-\alpha\cdot T_c)}{\exp(-\alpha\cdot T_c)+\sum_{m=1}^{n}\exp(-\alpha_m\cdot T_m)}\cdot (T_{cm}-T_c)\cdot c_t + \\ \qquad\qquad\qquad\qquad\qquad\qquad\qquad\qquad\qquad\qquad\qquad\qquad\qquad\qquad\\ c_o\cdot F\cdot \dfrac{1000}{D_l}\cdot \dfrac{1000}{D_s}\cdot\left(\dfrac{D_s}{v}+T_s\right)\cdot 2\right\} \quad (5\text{-}5)$$

Objective function O6, that is minimising total costs, is formulated as:

$$O6:\ MIN\left\{c_t\cdot T_c\cdot P + c_o\cdot F\cdot \dfrac{1000}{D_l}\cdot \dfrac{1000}{D_s}\cdot\left(\dfrac{D_s}{v}+T_s\right)\cdot 2\right\} \quad (5\text{-}6)$$

Finally objective function O7, maximising patronage, is given by:

$$O7:\ MAX\left\{P_0\cdot \dfrac{\exp(-\alpha\cdot T_c)}{\exp(-\alpha\cdot T_c)+\sum_{m=1}^{n}\exp(-\alpha_m\cdot T_m)}\right\} \quad (5\text{-}7)$$

5.4 Discussion

Seven objectives have been defined, using the perspectives of the three parties involved in network design. Each of these objectives is formulated using the building blocks presented in Chapter 4, as is shown in Table 5-1.

Each objective function represents a dilemma between opposing factors:

- O1: Minimise weighted travel time: short access time is to be balanced versus short in-vehicle time;
- O2: Minimise weighted travel time under a fixed budget: short access time versus short in vehicle time, and short access time versus short waiting time;
- O3: Maximise cost effectiveness: high patronage versus low operational costs;
- O4: Maximise operator's profit: high patronage versus low operational costs;
- O5: Maximise social welfare: net user's benefit versus net operator's benefit;
- O6: Minimise total costs: low travel times versus low operational costs.
- O7: Maximise total passengers: short access time versus short in-vehicle time.

Table 5-1: Overview of objectives and building blocks

Objective	Max/Min	1 Total travel time	2 Access time	3 In-vehicle time	4 Waiting time	5 Frequency	6 Patronage	7 Operational costs	8 Revenues	9 Consumer	10 Total travel costs	11 Total costs
O1: Travel time	Min	X	X	X	O							
O2: Travel time (fixed budget)	Min	X	X	X	X	X						
O3: Cost effectiveness	Max	X	X	X	X			X	X	X		
O4: Operator's profit	Max	X	X	X	X			X	X	X		
O5: Social welfare	Max	X	X	X	O			X	X	X	X	
O6: Total costs	Min	X	X	X	O		O	X			X	X
O7: Total passengers	Max	X	X	X	X		X					

Note: X: required, O: optional

This description of the objective functions using the building blocks or using the dilemmas leads to following observations:

- Building block BB5, describing the frequency, is only used in objective function O2: minimising travel time under a fixed budget. All other objectives assume that the frequency is fixed. O2 might therefore be used to improve the performance of a network once the operational costs have been determined using one of the other objective functions, for instance O6;

- Objective functions O1 and O7, i.e. minimising travel time and maximising patronage respectively, are concerned with the same dilemma: access time versus in-vehicle time. Given the demand models of equations 4-7 and 4-8, the results will be identical. Since O1 has already been qualified as rather naive, the same qualification might hold for objective function O7;

- Since the travel-time-ratio defined in equation 4-9, does not incorporate weights for the time elements, the combination of O7 and 4-9 will result in different solutions compared to O1. However, this result can also be analysed using O1 by setting all weights equal to 1;

- Objective functions O3 and O4, maximising cost effectiveness and maximising profit respectively, deal with a similar dilemma. In O3, however the ratio of revenue and costs is used, while in O4 the difference between revenue and costs is optimised. The ratio used in O3 has the disadvantage that in the case that the travel demand is less sensitive for changes in the network than the operational costs, no optimum can be found. O4 might therefore be a more robust objective;

- O6 has the interesting feature that it is possible to assume a fixed demand level.

Chapter 5 Objective functions for public transport network design

There is an interesting similarity between the objective functions O5 and O6. O5 can be simplified as follows:

$$MAX\{0.5 \cdot P(T_c) \cdot (T_{cm} - T_c) \cdot c_t + (r_t + r_s) \cdot P(T_c) - C_o\} \quad (5-8)$$

If Equation (5-8) is multiplied by -1, the resulting equation must be minimised:

$$MIN\left\{\left(0.5 \cdot T_c - 0.5 \cdot T_{cm} - \frac{(r_t + r_s)}{c_t}\right) \cdot P(T_c) \cdot c_t + C_o\right\} \quad (5-9)$$

Comparison of Equation (5-9) with Equation (5-6), or better (4-17), shows that T_c in objective function O6 is replaced by the term:

$$0.5 \cdot T_c - 0.5 \cdot T_{cm} - \frac{(r_t + r_s)}{c_t} = 0.5 \cdot T_c - \varepsilon \quad (5-10)$$

This equation shows that, compared to minimising total costs, maximising social welfare will be less sensitive for changes in travel time due to the factor 0.5 and the constant ε, which will generally be large because of the value of T_{cm}.

5.5 Selection of promising objectives

Given these remarks it may be concluded that the objective functions O4, maximising operator's profit, O5, maximising social welfare, and O6, minimising total costs, are the most realistic objective functions for the network design problem.

O2, minimising travel time on a fixed operational budget, might be used to improve the quality of the network given the constraints derived using for instance objective function O6, minimising total costs. In this case, two strategies can be followed. The simplest strategy is solving objective function O6 and using the optimal values for stop spacing and line spacing to calculate the operational costs. These costs can then be used as a design parameter in objective function O2, minimising travel time on a fixed budget, resulting in new optimal values for the optimal stop and line spacing. The second possibility is to use objective function O6 and to solve it for three decision variables simultaneously, that is, stop spacing, line spacing, and frequency. Since the focus of this report is on stop spacing and line spacing only, this second approach will be studied for theoretical purposes only, and will not be applied to specific cases.

Chapter 6

SOLVING OPTIMISATION MODELS

As stated in Chapter 3, there are two basic methods to find optimal values for stop spacing and line spacing: analytical approach and enumeration. Given an objective function, the optimum values for the decision variables can be determined by setting the partial derivatives with respect to the decision variables equal to zero, and by solving these equations. In the case of complicated objective functions, enumeration is an alternative approach. With enumeration the value of the objective function is calculated for a systematic set of values for the decision variables, and the set having the best value for the objective function is selected. In this chapter both approaches are used. All objective functions are solved using enumeration, and objective functions that are mathematically tractable, that is, objective functions where it is assumed that the demand level is fixed, are solved analytically.

6.1 O1: Minimising weighted travel time

For objective O1 the objective function to minimise is (see Equation (5-1)):

$$O1 = w_a \cdot \frac{f_a \cdot (D_s + D_l)}{v_a} + w_w \cdot \frac{f_w}{F} + \frac{D_c}{D_s} \cdot \left(\frac{D_s}{v} + T_s\right) + w_e \cdot T_e \qquad (6\text{-}1)$$

Given the assumption that D_l and F are fixed, this objective of the weighted total travel time has its minimum where the first derivative with respect to D_s equals 0:

$$\frac{dO1}{dD_s} = \frac{w_a \cdot f_a}{v_a} - \frac{D_c \cdot T_s}{D_s^2} = 0 \qquad (6\text{-}2)$$

From (6-2) it follows that the optimal stop spacing is given by:

$$D_s^* = \sqrt{\frac{v_a \cdot D_c \cdot T_s}{w_a \cdot f_a}} \qquad (6\text{-}3)$$

Expression (6-3) shows that the optimal stop spacing increases with access speed, travel distance, maximum speed of the vehicle, and time lost at the stop respectively, whereas the weight of access time has a reverse influence on optimal stop spacing.

For illustrative purposes it is useful to simplify the objective as follows:

$$O1 = \kappa \cdot D_s + \frac{\lambda}{D_s} + \mu \qquad (6\text{-}4)$$

where:

$$\kappa = \frac{w_a \cdot f_a}{v_a}$$

$$\lambda = D_c \cdot T_s$$

$$\mu = \frac{w_w \cdot f_w}{F} + \frac{D_c}{v} + w_e \cdot T_e$$

κ can be seen as the access factor, λ as the stop loss factor, and μ represents the fixed trip time elements, that is, the in-vehicle time without stops, the waiting time, and the egress time.

The optimal stop spacing then is determined by:

$$\frac{dO1}{dD_s} = \kappa - \frac{\lambda}{D_s^2} = 0 \qquad (6\text{-}5)$$

leading to:

$$D_s^{*2} = \frac{\lambda}{\kappa} = \frac{v_a \cdot D_c \cdot T_s}{w_a \cdot f_a} = \frac{\lambda'}{\kappa} \cdot D_c \qquad (6\text{-}6)$$

where:

$$\lambda' = T_s$$

Expression (6-4) shows the conflicting influence of access time ($\kappa \cdot D_s$) and the variable part of the in-vehicle time (λ/D_s). The fixed part of the in-vehicle time is included in the term μ. The graphical representation of this conflict, as shown in Figure 6-1 illustrates two interesting characteristics of the model.

First, the objective function O1 proves to be flat. Even large deviations from the optimal stop spacing will result in rather small changes in the value of the objective function O1. The implication of the shallow objective is that optimal stop spacing should not be used as a rigid design variable but that allowances can be made for specific local situations.

Chapter 6 Solving optimisation models 41

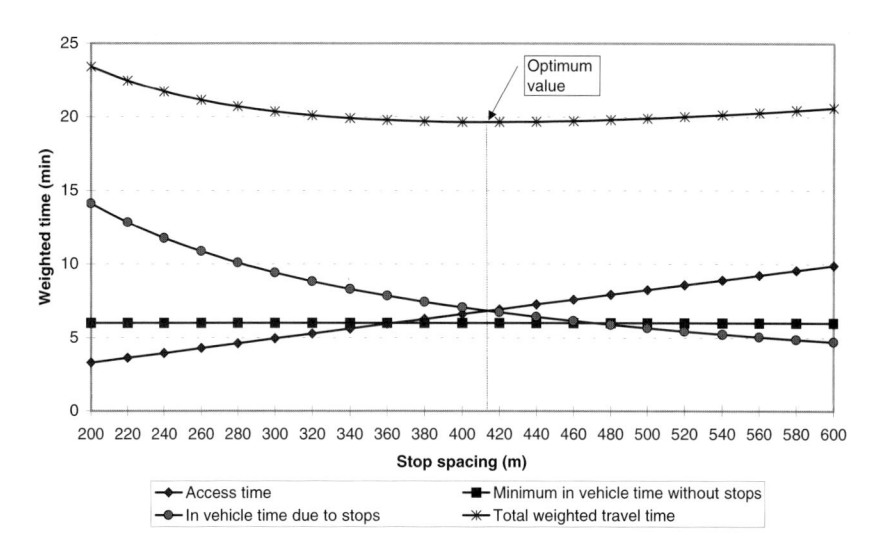

Figure 6-1: O1: Minimising weighted total door-to-door travel time

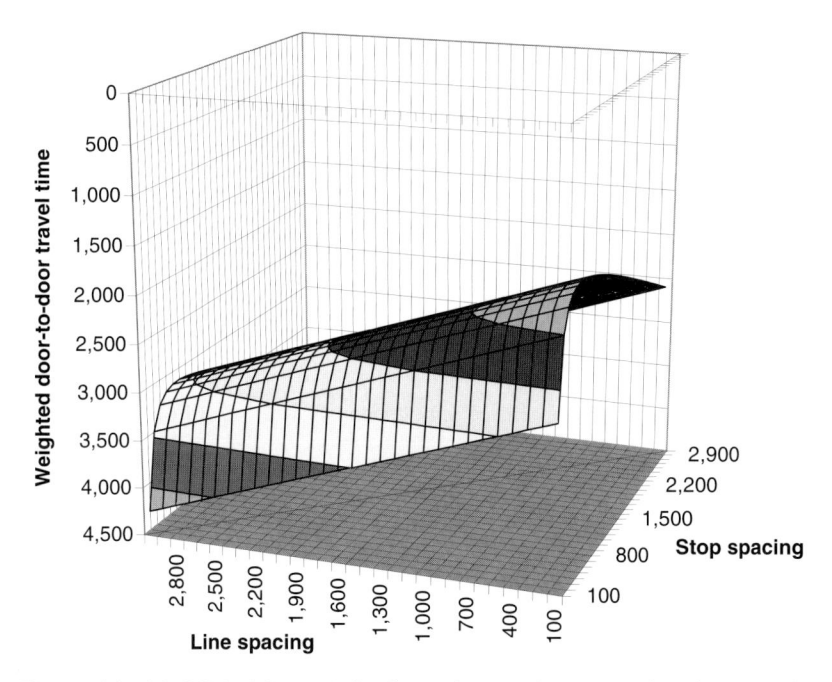

Figure 6-2: O1: Minimising weighted travel time (please note that the vertical axis is reversed)

Second, the optimum is located at the intersection of the functions for the access time and the time lost due to stops. It can easily be shown that this relationship, which has also been found by other researchers (e.g. Holroyd (1967), Kocur & Hendrickson (1982), Tsao & Schonfeld (1983), and Spasovic & Schonfeld (1993)), holds for every objective that can be formulated as formula (6-4): solving Equation (6-5) yields the same solution as solving Equation (6-7):

$$\kappa \cdot D_s = \frac{\lambda}{D_s} \tag{6-7}$$

Figure 6-2 shows the shape of the objective functions in the case that enumeration is used. Travel time increases as line spacing increases, and for each value of the line spacing the optimal stop spacing is identical. Furthermore, it is clear that smaller values of the stop spacing have more influence on the value of the objective function than larger values.

6.2 O2: Minimising weighted travel time on a fixed budget

The objective function O2 is again the sum of access time, waiting time, and riding time In this case, however, the frequency is not assumed to be fixed, but is determined by the available budget, the stop spacing and the line spacing. As a matter of fact, in objective function O2 there is a trade-off between access time and waiting time too: large access times results into higher frequencies and vice versa. The objective function can be written as:

$$O2 = w_a \cdot \frac{f_a \cdot (D_s + D_l)}{v_a} + w_w \cdot \frac{f_w \cdot c_o}{B_o} \cdot \frac{1000}{D_l} \cdot \frac{1000}{D_s} \cdot \left(\frac{D_s}{v} + T_s\right) \cdot 2 + \frac{D_c}{D_s} \cdot \left(\frac{D_s}{v} + T_s\right) + w_e \cdot T_{we} \tag{6-8}$$

Objective function (6-8) can be optimised simultaneously with regard to stop spacing D_s and line spacing D_l, leading to:

$$\begin{cases} D_s^{*2} = \frac{\lambda'}{\kappa} \cdot \left(\frac{\tau}{D_l^*} + D_c\right) & (6\text{-}9a) \\ \\ D_l^{*2} = \frac{\lambda'}{\kappa} \cdot \left(\frac{\tau}{D_s^*} + \frac{\tau}{\lambda' \cdot v}\right) & (6\text{-}9b) \end{cases}$$

where:

$$\kappa = \frac{w_a \cdot f_a}{v_a}$$

$$\lambda' = T_s$$

$$\tau = \frac{w_w \cdot f_w \cdot 1000^2 \cdot 2 \cdot c_o}{B_o}$$

τ represents the waiting time factor. Both Equations (6-9a) and (6-9b) have a similar structure as Equation (6-6), that is, the structure resulting when Equation (6-4) is optimised. This would imply that, correspondingly, the relationship found previously would still hold, namely that at the optimum value of the objective function, the values of access costs, costs lost due to stops, and waiting costs should all be equal.

There is, however, an important difference, which calls for some nuance. Both derivatives contain a part that relates to the access costs. The derivative with respect to D_s, however, is concerned only with the component of the access costs parallel to the line, whereas the derivative with respect to D_l is concerned only with the component of the access costs perpendicular to the line. The part of the access costs perpendicular to the line should therefore equal the waiting costs while the component parallel to the line should equal the sum of the in-vehicle costs and that part of the waiting costs that depends on the stop spacing.

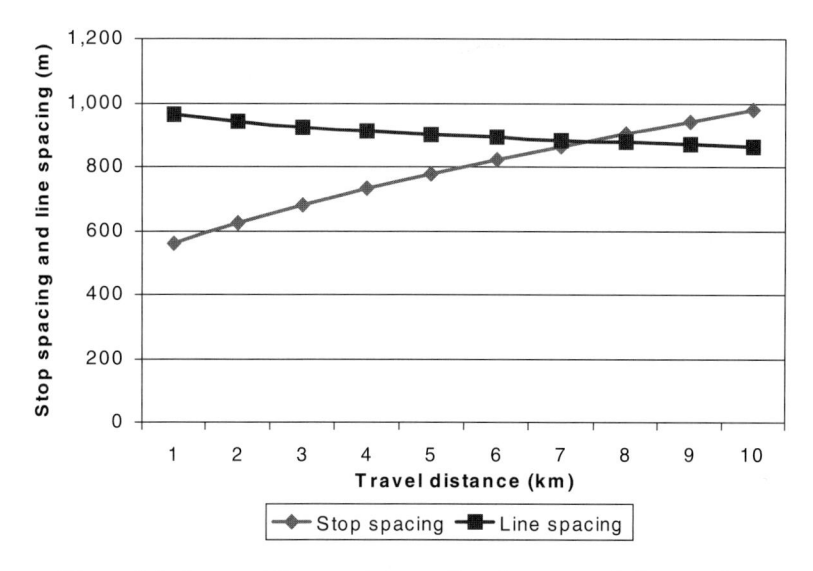

Figure 6-3: Stop and line spacing as a function of travel distance D_c

A comparison of Equations (6-3) and (6-9a) shows that objective O2 has similar characteristics as objective O1. The stop spacing has still a square root relationship with the travel distance, but because of the introduction of the line spacing this relationship is less strong. Equation (6-9b) shows that in an urban corridor the optimal line spacing is only weakly dependent on the travel distance. An increase of the travel distance will lead to an increase of the optimal stop spacing, which will result in a decrease of the line spacing, as can be seen in Figure 6-3.

The shape of the objective function is show in Figure 6-4. It clearly shows that there is a large range of values for stop spacing and line spacing where the values of the objective function are more or less equal.

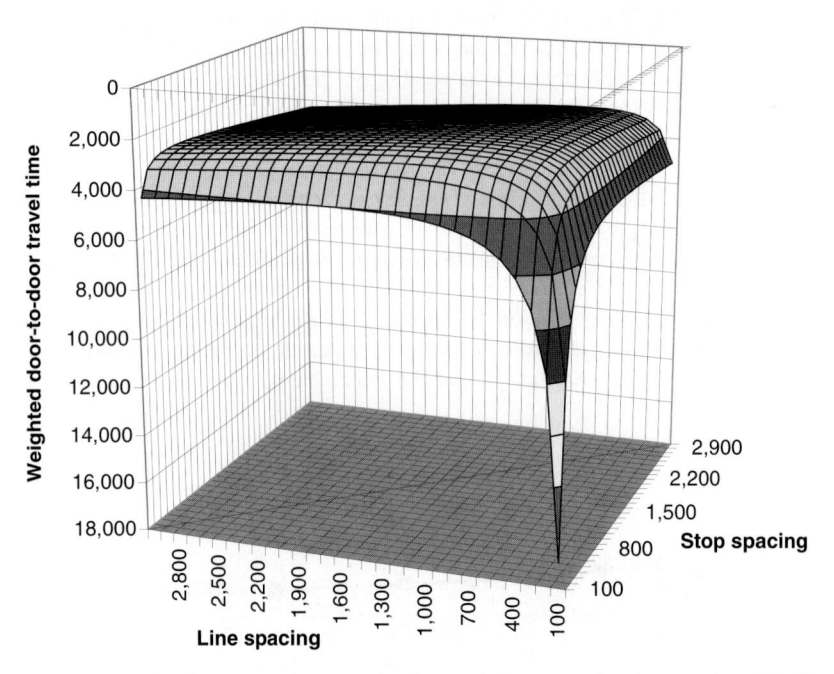

Figure 6-4: O2: Minimising weighted travel time on a fixed operational budget (please note that the vertical axis is reversed)

6.3 O3: Maximising cost efficiency

The shape of objective function O3, maximising cost effectiveness, is shown in Figure 6-5. In this case the logit-mode-choice model is used. As can be seen, this objective function does not result in optimal values for stop spacing and line spacing. Large line spacing always results in a higher cost efficiency. This is caused by the fact that the demand for public transport is relatively inelastic. Since the operational costs are in the denominator, a reduction of operational costs leads always to a higher cost efficiency. There is, however, a small range of values for the stop spacing where, given a specific line spacing, the cost effectiveness is optimal. This range varies between 1,900 and 2,400 metres.

Chapter 6 Solving optimisation models

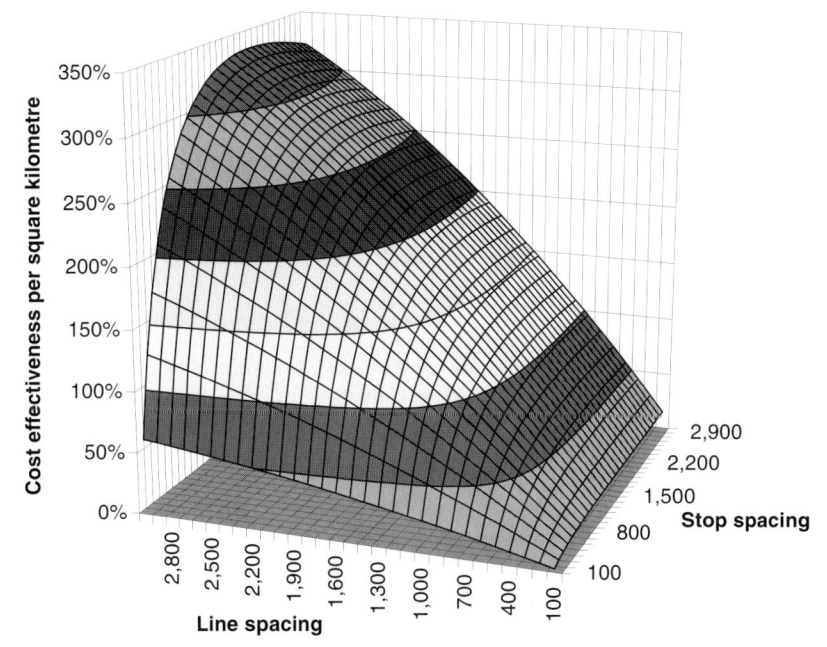

Figure 6-5: O3: Maximising cost effectiveness

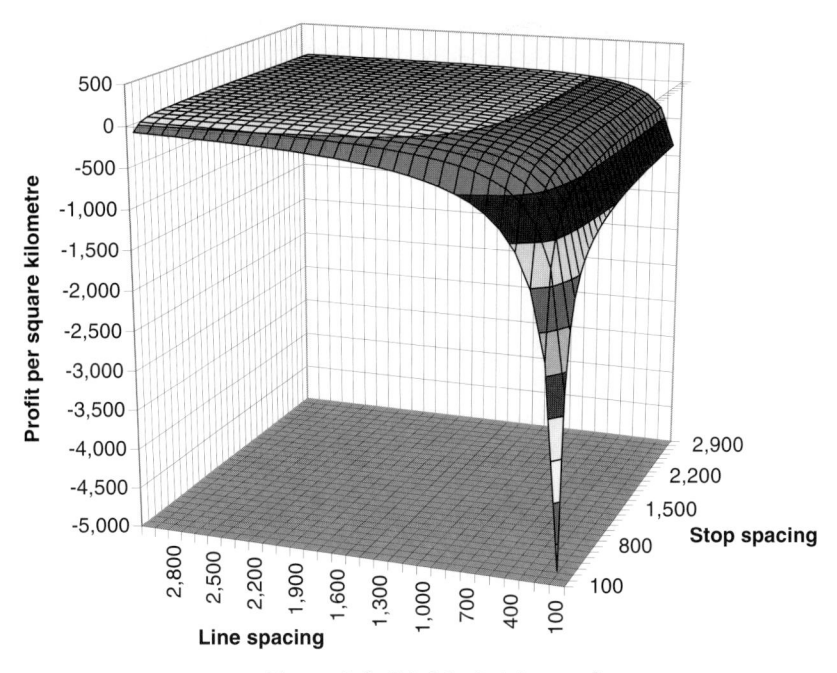

Figure 6-6: O4: Maximising profit

6.4 O4: Maximising profit

As expected, objective function O4, maximising operator's profit, results in an optimum. Furthermore, from Figure 6-6. it is clear that there is a large range of values of the design variables where the profit is more or less equal.

6.5 O5: Maximising social welfare

Objective function O5, maximising social welfare, has a similar shape as minimising travel time given an operational budget, and maximising profit (see Figure 6-7). The main difference is that it is easier to see that there is an optimum. Again, there is a large range of values for the stop spacing and line spacing for which the value of the objective function is more or less equal.

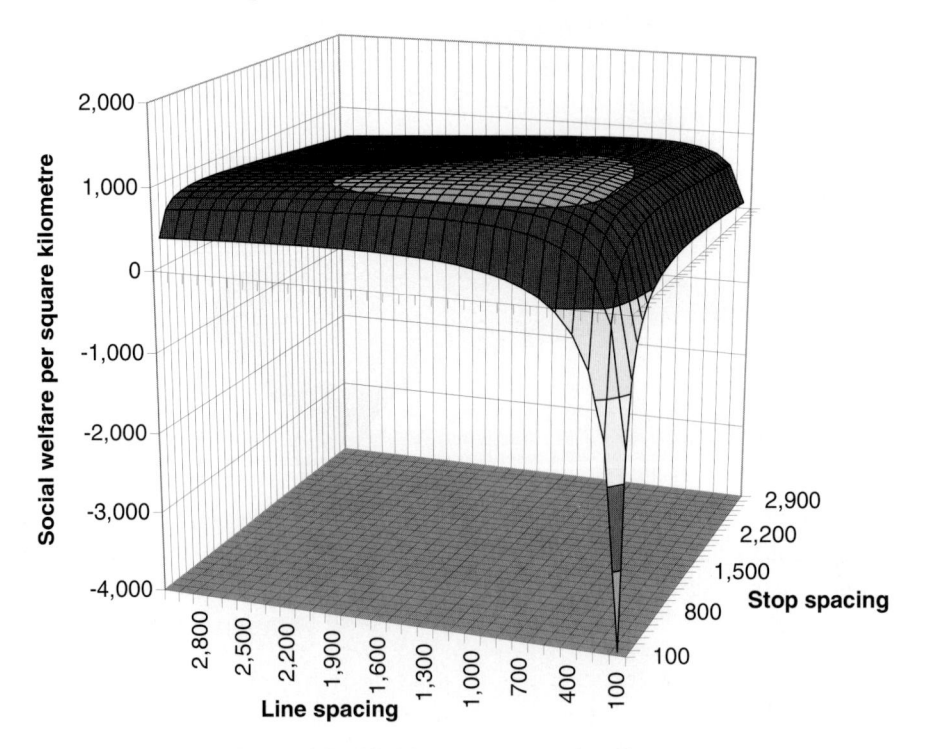

Figure 6-7: O5: Maximising social welfare

6.6 O6: Minimising total costs

6.6.1 Assuming a fixed demand level

In the case of a fixed demand level, objective function O6 can be solved analytically. Objective function O6 yields the following expression for the simultaneous choice of optimal stop and line spacing:

$$O6 = \left\{ w_a \cdot \frac{f_a \cdot (D_s + D_l)}{v_a} + w_w \cdot \frac{f_w}{F} + \frac{D_c}{D_s} \cdot \left(\frac{D_s}{v} + T_s \right) + w_e \cdot T_e \right\} \cdot P \cdot c_t + \\ F \cdot \frac{1000}{D_l} \cdot \frac{1000}{D_s} \cdot \left(\frac{D_s}{v} + T_s \right) \cdot 2 \cdot c_o \quad (6\text{-}10)$$

This objective function has a minimum if the first derivatives with respect to D_s and to D_l both equal 0, which leads to:

$$\begin{cases} D_s^{*2} = \dfrac{\lambda'}{\kappa} \cdot \left(\dfrac{\rho}{D_l^*} + D_c \right) & (6\text{-}11a) \\[2ex] D_l^{*2} = \dfrac{\lambda'}{\kappa} \cdot \left(\dfrac{\rho}{D_s^*} + \dfrac{\rho}{\lambda' \cdot v} \right) & (6\text{-}11b) \end{cases}$$

where:

$$\kappa = \frac{w_a \cdot f_a}{v_a}$$

$$\lambda' = T_s$$

$$\rho = \frac{F \cdot 1000^2 \cdot c_o \cdot 2}{P \cdot c_t}$$

In this formulation ρ can be seen as the trade-off factor between traveller's and operator's costs. The component of the access costs perpendicular to the line should equal the operational costs and the part of the access costs parallel to the line should equal the sum of the in-vehicle costs and that part of the operational costs that depends on the stop spacing. The optimal stop spacing again has a square root relationship with the travel distance, while the line spacing, again, only weakly depends on the travel distance. The relationships are similar to those shown in Figure 6-3.

6.6.2 Using the logit-mode-choice model

The shape of objective function O6, minimising total costs, using a logit-mode-choice model is illustrated in Figure 6-8. This objective function, again, shows a large range of values for stop and line spacing resulting in more or less identical values for the objective function. In this case to, it is less clear to see whether there is an optimum. As a matter of fact, in the case that the logit-elasticity model is used, the shape of the objective function is still similar, however, no optimum is found. The reason for this is that when the demand is sensitive for changes in the service quality, which is the case using the logit-elasticity model, an increase in travel time is more than compensated by the reduction of travellers. As a result the net costs for travelling will be reduced as well as the operational costs, leading to a lower value for the objective to be minimised. It might therefore be concluded that for this objective function, a fixed demand level should be assumed.

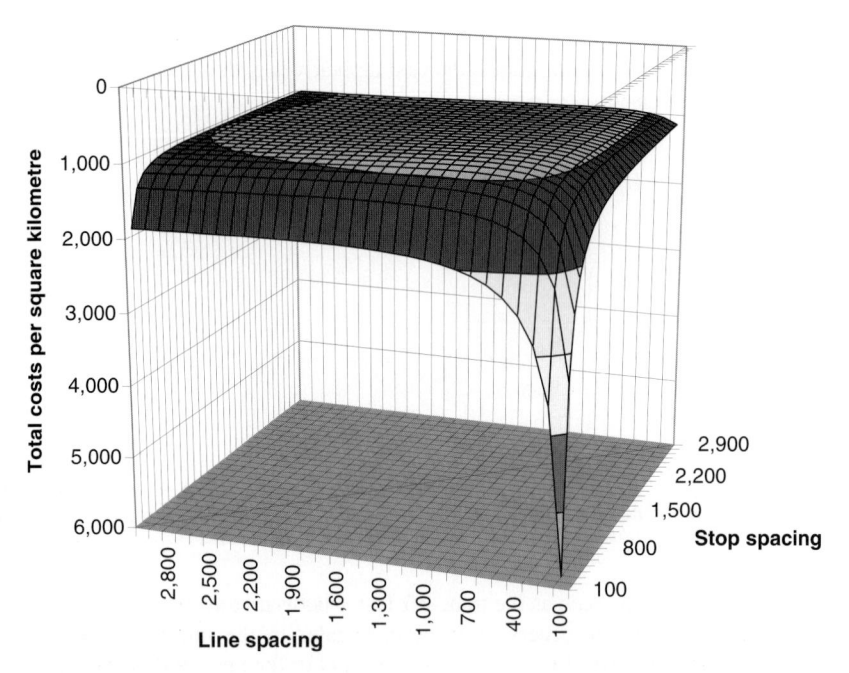

Figure 6-8: O6: Minimising total costs (please note that the vertical axis is reversed)

6.6.3 Solving for stop spacing, line spacing, and frequency simultaneously

In Section 5.5 it was suggested that objective O2, minimising weighted travel time given a fixed operational budget, might be used to improve the solution found using objective O6, minimising total costs. A possible approach is to optimise objective function O6 for three decision variables simultaneously: stop spacing, line spacing, and frequency. This implies that the derivatives of objective O6, Equation (6-10), with respect to stop spacing,

Chapter 6 Solving optimisation models   49

line spacing, and frequency should all equal 0. This yields the following set of equations, which can be solved using a Gauss-Seidel iteration scheme:

$$\begin{cases} D_s^{*2} = \dfrac{\lambda'}{\kappa} \cdot \left(\dfrac{\rho' \cdot F^*}{D_l^*} + D_c \right) & \text{(6-12a)} \\[2ex] D_l^{*2} = \dfrac{\lambda'}{\kappa} \cdot \left(\dfrac{\rho'}{D_s^*} + \dfrac{\rho'}{\lambda' \cdot v} \right) \cdot F^* & \text{(6-12b)} \\[2ex] F^{*2} = \dfrac{\tau'}{\lambda'} \cdot \left(\dfrac{1}{\dfrac{\rho'}{D_s^*} + \dfrac{\rho'}{\lambda' \cdot v}} \right) \cdot D_l^* & \text{(6-12c)} \end{cases}$$

where:

$$\kappa = \frac{w_a \cdot f_a}{v_a}$$

$$\lambda' = T_s$$

$$\rho' = \frac{1000^2 \cdot c_o \cdot 2}{P \cdot c_t}$$

$$\tau' = w_w \cdot f_w$$

6.7 O7: Maximising patronage

As expected, objective function O7, maximising travel demand, does not result in an optimum (see Figure 6-9). A decrease in line spacing leads always to an increase in patronage. Given a specific line spacing, however, the optimal stop spacing can be found. As stated earlier, this optimum coincides with the optimum for O1, that is minimising travel time.

Figure 6-10 and Figure 6-11 shows the influence of other descriptions of the travel demand using Equations (4-8) or (4-9) on O7, maximising travel demand. Using these models, the level of travel demand is generally more sensitive to changes in the service quality than using the logit-mode-choice model of Equation (4-7).

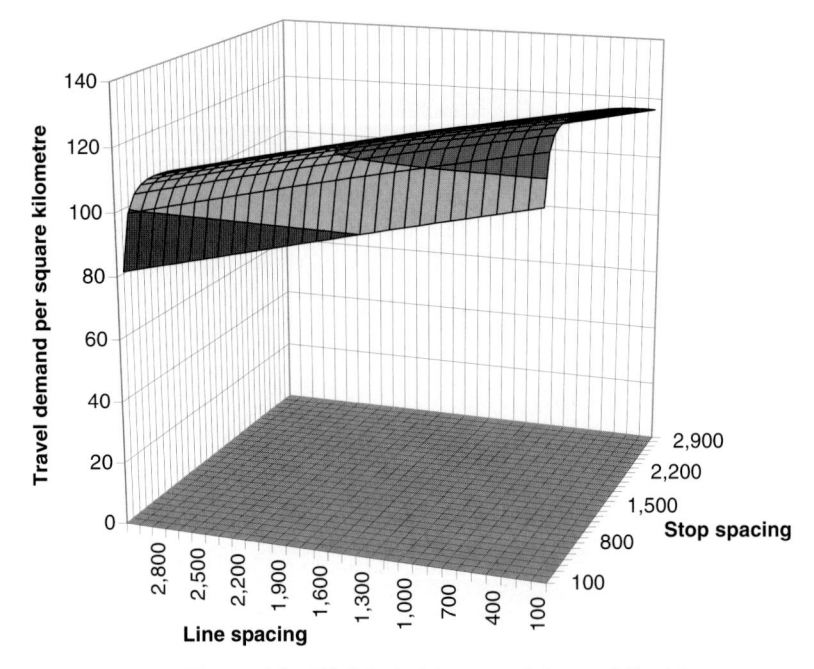

Figure 6-9: O7: Maximising travel demand (logit)

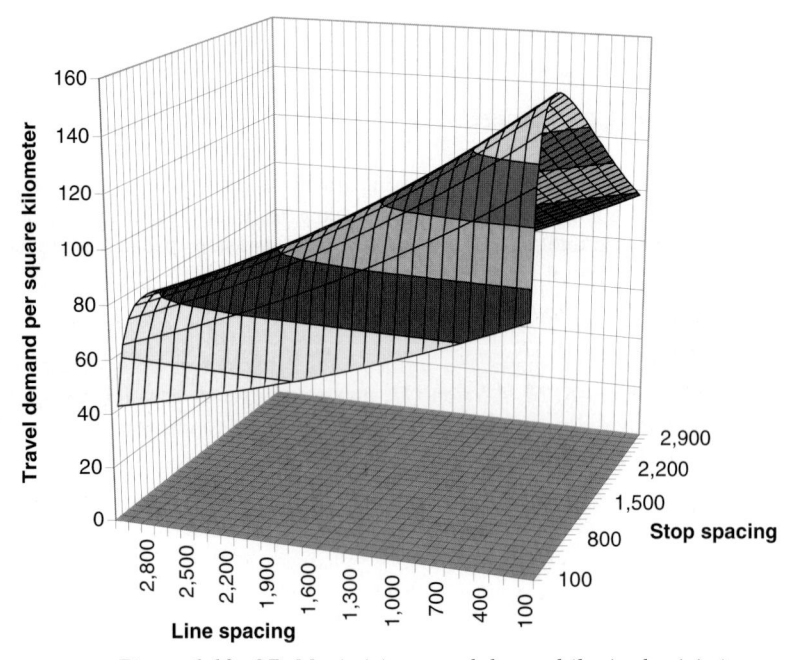

Figure 6-10: O7: Maximising travel demand (logit-elasticity)

Chapter 6 Solving optimisation models   51

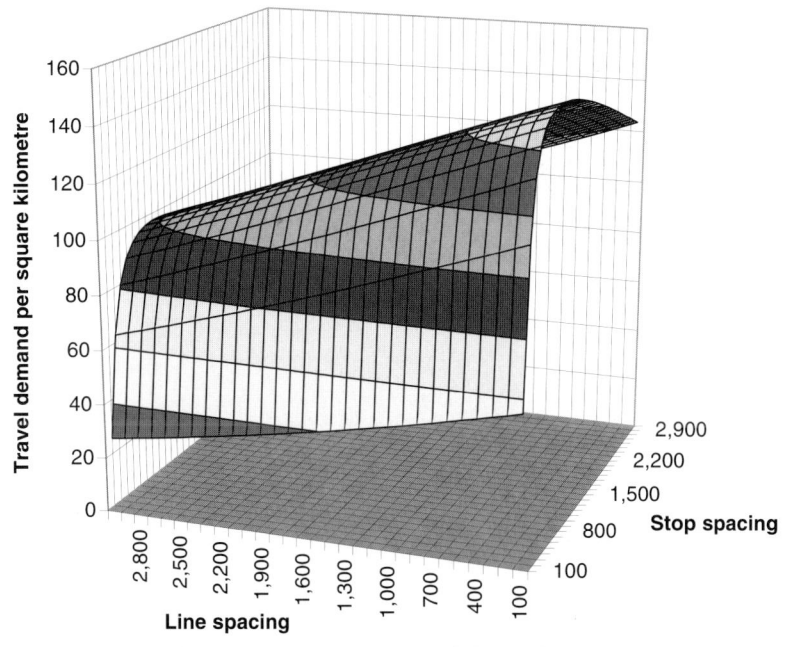

Figure 6-11: O7: Maximising travel demand (travel-time-ratio)

6.8 Conclusions

The analysis presented above leads to the following conclusions.

First, the line of reasoning used in the selection of objectives in Section 5.5 is confirmed. The objectives of maximising operator's profit (O4), maximising social welfare (O5), and minimising total (O6) costs were shown to lead to optimal solutions, while objectives such as minimising weighted travel time (O1), maximising cost efficiency (O3), and maximising patronage (O7) yielded only optimal solutions in the case that a fixed line spacing was assumed. Given an operational budget, minimising weighted travel time (O2) might be a suitable objective too. For the objective of minimising total costs, however, it was found that a fixed demand level should be assumed in order to guarantee an optimal solution.

Second, it is shown that the main relationships for the decision variables can be described using square root functions. This mathematical relationship, and the shapes of the objective functions too, implies that the objective functions are rather flat near the optimum. This finding allows planners, for instance, to vary the stop spacing depending on local circumstances. Furthermore, this type of relationship indicates that a larger stop spacing, or line spacing, has less effect on the value of the objective function than a shorter stop spacing or line spacing.

Chapter 7

NUMERICAL RESULTS

In this chapter the optimisation models presented in the previous chapters will be applied to two typical situations: an urban bus network and an urban tram network respectively. Furthermore, a sensitivity analysis is presented for the main parameters used.

7.1 Characteristics of the analysis

The two situations studied are (see also Figure 7-1):

- A corridor in a bus network for a small city. The average trip length is 3 kilometres. A typical example are the neighbourhoods Zuilen/Overvecht in the city of Utrecht in the Netherlands, having an average stop spacing of 350 metres and a line spacing of 500 metres;
- A corridor in a tram network for a large city. The average trip length is 5 kilometres. An example of such an area is the southern part of the city of The Hague in the Netherlands, having an average stop spacing 400 metres and a line spacing of 1.000 metres.

Traditional bus   Traditional tram

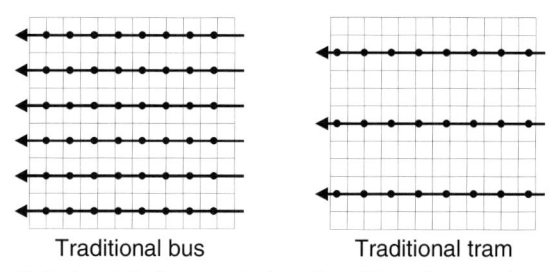

Figure 7-1: Spatial characteristics of traditional network structures

The values of all parameters used are given in Table 7-1. The derivation of the cost factors can be found in Appendix B. It should be noted that the level of demand that is assumed, is representative for an average peak hour.

Table 7-1: Values of the parameters used

Parameter	Symbol	Bus	Tram	Units
Travel distance	D_c	3,000	5,000	m
Access speed	v_a	1.1	1.1	m/s
Factor access distance	f_a	0.25	0.25	
Maximum speed public transport	v	13.9	13.9	m/s
Time lost at stops	T_s	34	34	s
Waiting time	T_w	450	300	s
Egress time	T_e	180	180	s
Regular frequency	F	4	6	veh/h
Fare	r_{tk}	0.25	0.25	fl/km
Subsidy	r_{sk}	0	0	fl/km
Operating costs per vehicle	c_o	217.35	362.25	fl/h
Weight access time	w_a	2.2	2.2	
Weight waiting time	w_w	1.5	1.5	
Weight egress time	w_e	1.1	1.1	
Value of time travellers	c_t	10.00	10.00	fl/h
Travel demand per square kilometre (fixed)	P	100	125	pas/km^2
Coefficient public transport (logit-models)	α	0.03	0.03	min^{-1}
Coefficient private car (logit-mode-choice)	α_m	0.08	0.08	min^{-1}
Average speed private car (logit-mode-choice)		4.2	4.2	m/s
Parking penalty (logit-mode-choice)		300	300	s
Reference access time (logit-elasticity)		300	300	s
Reference speed public transport (logit-elasticity)		5.6	6.9	m/s
Reference waiting time (logit-elasticity)		450	300	s

The results for the selected objectives include network characteristics such as stop spacing and line spacing, and performance characteristics such as travel times, operational costs, total costs, patronage, and so on. Some of these performance characteristics are also presented as averages per traveller, for instance, operational costs per traveller, which is equivalent to operational costs per trip. For reasons of comparison,

Chapter 7 Numerical results 55

the traditional network design values often found in the Netherlands, and the results for the simple model O1, minimising travel time only, are included too.

In the objective functions in which a variable level of demand is assumed, travel demand has been modelled using all three models presented in Section 4.3. The tables and figures, however, only present the results using the logit-mode-choice model, Equation (4-7). The results for the other demand models, that is logit-elasticity, Equation (4-8), and travel-time-ratio, Equation (4-9), respectively are discussed separately in Section 7.4.3. For objective function O6, minimising total costs, two cases are distinguished: assuming variable demand level (O6.1) and assuming a fixed level of demand (O6.2). Objective function O2, minimising travel time given a fixed budget, is used to improve the network given the operating budget found using O6.2 (fixed demand level) using the stepwise procedure described in Section 5.5.

7.2 Bus network

The typical traditional bus network structure has an average stop spacing of 350 metres and a line spacing of about 500 metres. The results of the application of the chosen objectives to the bus network case (average trip length is 3 kilometre) are presented in Table 7-2. Figure 7-2 shows these findings as index figures relative to the traditional design values. It is easy to see that in all cases stop spacing and line spacing are increased, while in nearly all cases the operational characteristics decrease.

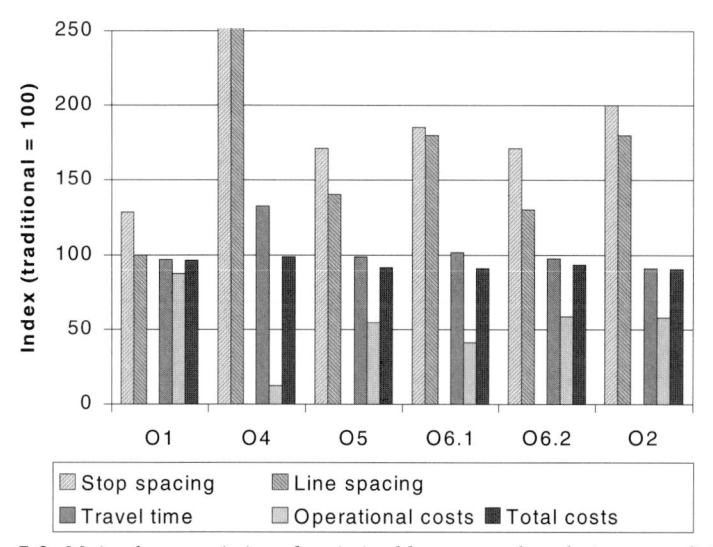

Figure 7-2: Main characteristics of optimised bus networks relative to traditional design

Table 7-2: Results of the selected objectives for a bus network (trip length: 3 kilometres)

	Traditional	O1: Min. Weighted Travel time	O4: Max. Profit	O5: Max. Social welfare	O6.1: Min. Costs	O6.2: Min. Costs	O2: Min. Weighted Travel time
Demand model		fixed	logit	logit	logit	fixed	fixed
Stop spacing *(m)*	350	450	1,000	600	650	600	700
Line spacing *(m)*	500	500	2,600	700	900	650	900
Stop density *(/km^2)*	5.7	4,4	0.4	2.4	1.7	2.6	1.6
Line density *(km/km^2)*	2.0	2.0	0.4	1.4	1.1	1.5	1.1
Frequency *(veh/h)*	4.0	4.0	4.0	4.0	4.0	4.0	5.9
Travel time *(min)*	22.1	21.4	29.3	21.8	22.5	21.6	20.1
Weighted travel time *(min)*	30.0	29.8	49.5	31.7	33.5	31.3	30.2
Operator costs *(fl/km^2)*	163	142	20	89	67	95	95
Cost effectiveness	46%	53%	294%	83%	108%	79%	79%
Profit *(fl/km^2)*	-88	-67	38	-15	5	-20	-20
Total costs *(fl/km^2)*	663	638	655	607	603	617	598
Patronage	100	100	77	98	96	100	100
Operational costs per traveller *(fl)*	1.63	1.42	0.26	0.90	0.69	0.95	0.95
Total costs per traveller *(fl)*	6.63	6.38	8.51	6.19	6.28	6.17	5.98

Note: Exogenous input values are shown in bold print. Adopted parameter values are given in Table 7-1.

Using the simple objective of minimising travel time only (O1) while keeping the line spacing fixed, already leads to an improvement of all performance characteristics.

The objective of profit maximisation (O4) results in a significant increase of travel times (up to 49.5 minutes), a loss of patronage (33 %), and, of course, an improvement of the operator performance characteristics. It should be noted that in this case the subsidy is assumed to be zero. The argument for this assumption is that the level of subsidy is arbitrary, unless it is determined using a societal objective such as minimising total costs, as modelled in objective O6.

Chapter 7 Numerical results 57

Maximising social welfare (O5) results in shorter travel times but higher weighted travel times. The demand for public transport drops with 2 % and operational costs are reduced significantly, more than 45 %. The linear approach of Equation (4-14) yields identical results.

Minimising total costs (O6.1) results in higher weighted travel times, a small loss of patronage (4 %) while the operator costs are reduced to about 40 % of the traditional costs. In the case that a fixed demand level is assumed, O6.2, the impact on the performance characteristics is smaller. The reduction in operational costs, however, is still more than 40 %.

The improvement of the network found using O2 results in larger stop spacing and line spacing, 700 and 900 metres, which enables frequencies of nearly 6 vehicles per hour. Given the budget reduction of 40 %, the weighted travel times are still about equal to those for the traditional network structure. This network also results in the lowest total costs per traveller.

The overall best solution is the results of objective O2, minimising travel time on a fixed budget, given the budget found using objective function O6.2, minimising travel costs. It has the lowest travel times and the lowest costs per traveller.

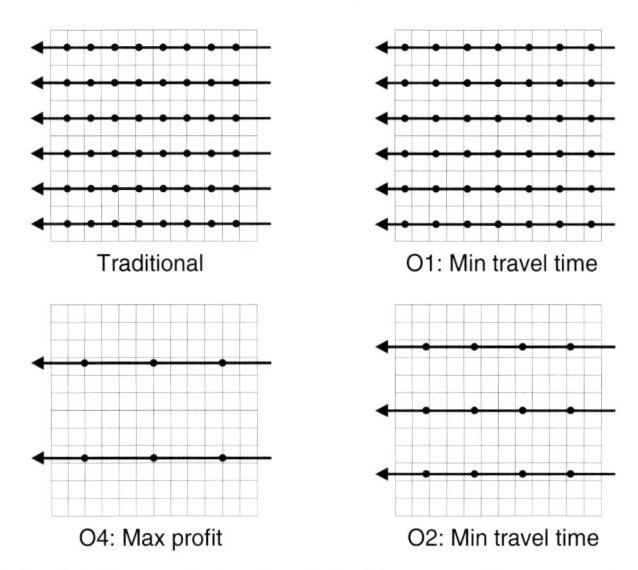

Figure 7-3: Spatial characteristics of optimised bus networks compared to traditional design

Figure 7-3 gives an impression of the impact of the various objectives on the spatial characteristics of the network. It clearly shows that the traditional network structure is too dense with regard to stop spacing as well as to line spacing.

Finally, the fact that in the overall best solution, O2, the frequency is significantly higher than 4 vehicles per hour, shows that time accessibility is more important than usually is assumed. Simultaneous optimisation of stop spacing, line spacing and frequency as described in Section 6.6.3 results in slightly higher values for stop spacing, line spacing, and frequency.

7.3 Tram network

The typical traditional tram network is characterised by an average stop spacing of 400 metres and a line spacing of about 1,000 metres. The analyses for a tram network (average trip length is 5 kilometres) show similar results as for the bus network (see Table 7-3 and Figure 7-4). Compared to traditional design, stop spacing increases in all cases. Line spacing, however, decreases slightly for most objectives. The performance characteristics show, again, a decrease for nearly all cases.

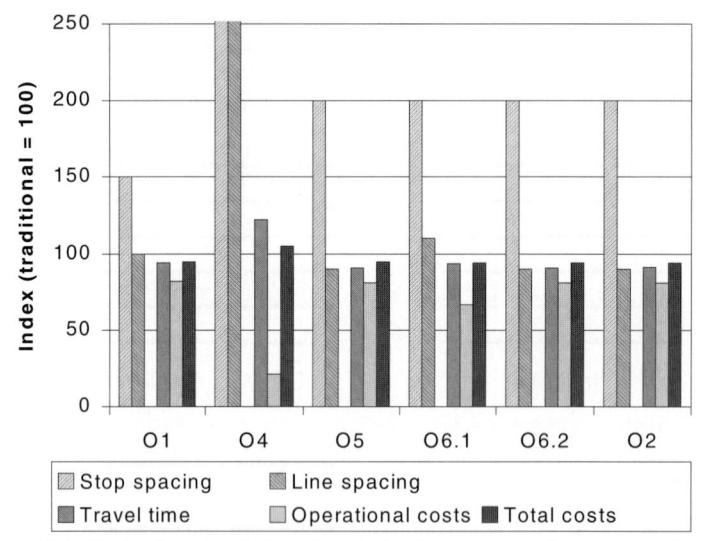

Figure 7-4: Main characteristics of optimised tram networks compared to traditional design

Analysis of Figure 7-4 and Table 7-3 leads to the following findings:

- The use of the simple objective (O1) already results in an improvement of the performance characteristics;
- Profit maximisation (O4) again results in networks having low densities and high travel times;
- Maximising social welfare (O5) leads to more attractive travel times and a reduction of the operator costs by 15 %;

Chapter 7 Numerical results

- Minimising total costs results in an equally attractive performance (O6.1), or, in the case that a fixed demand is assumed (O6.2), in even more attractive travel times, while the operator costs are reduced by more than 15 %. In the latter case the results are identical to maximising social welfare (O5).

Table 7-3: Results of the selected objectives for a tram network (trip length: 5 kilometres)

	Traditional	O1: Min. Weighted Travel time	O4: Max. Profit	O5: Max. Social welfare	O6.1: Min. Costs	O6.2: Min. Costs	O2: Min. Weighted Travel time
Demand model		fixed	logit	logit	logit	fixed	fixed
Stop spacing *(m)*	**400**	**600**	1,200	800	800	800	800
Line spacing *(m)*	**1,000**	**1,000**	3,000	900	1,100	900	900
Stop density *(/km²)*	**2.5**	1.7	0.3	1.4	1.1	1.4	1.4
Line density *(km/km²)*	**1.0**	**1.0**	0.3	1.1	0.9	1.1	1.1
Frequency *(veh/h)*	**6.0**	**6.0**	**6.0**	**6.0**	**6.0**	**6.0**	6.0
Travel time *(min)*	26.3	24.7	32.1	23.9	24.7	23.9	23.9
Weighted travel time *(min)*	35.4	34.7	53.8	34.4	36.0	34.4	34.4
Operator costs *(fl/km²)*	189	155	40	153	126	153	**153**
Cost effectiveness	83%	101%	322%	103%	123%	102%	102%
Profit *(fl/km²)*	-33	1	90	4	29	3	3
Total costs *(fl/km²)*	927	878	973	875	870	869	869
Patronage	**125**	**125**	104	126	124	**125**	125
Operational costs per traveller *(fl)*	1.51	1.24	0.39	1.22	1.01	1.23	1.22
Total costs per traveller *(fl)*	7.42	7.03	9.36	6.94	7.01	6.95	6.95

Note: Exogenous input values are shown in bold print. Adopted parameter values are given in Table 7-1.

It is interesting to see that the result of O6.2 with regard to the weighted travel times could not be improved by changing the frequency using O2. Apparently, a frequency of 6 vehicles per hour is optimal. It is, again, this network that results in the lowest overall costs per traveller. Simultaneous optimisation of stop spacing, line spacing, and frequency results in more or less identical values as those found using objective O2.

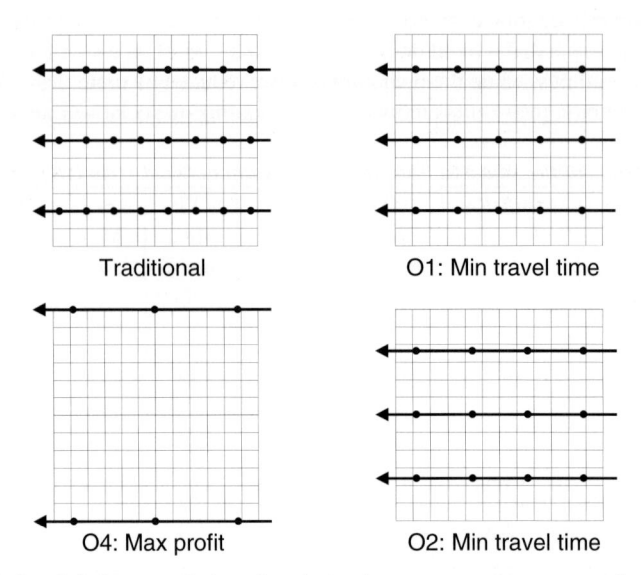

Figure 7-5: Spatial characteristics of optimised tram networks compared to traditional design

Finally, Figure 7-5 gives an impression of the spatial consequences of the various objectives for tram networks. It clearly shows that the stop spacing in traditional network structures are too short.

7.4 Sensitivity analysis

The numerical results presented in the previous sections are, of course, strongly influenced by the values of the design and system parameters as presented in Table 7-1. The question then is what the sensitivity is for the assumptions that have been made.
This section focuses first on the objective function of minimising total costs, under the assumption of a fixed demand level (O6.2), which has been solved analytically. Second, attention is paid to other objective functions: minimising weighted travel time given a fixed operational budget (O2), maximising profit (O4), and maximising social welfare (O5). Finally, it is discussed how the way transport demand is modelled, influences the results.

7.4.1 Sensitivity for O6.2: Minimising total costs

The analytical approach presented in Section 6.6.1 showed five key input factors for objective function O6.2 (see the factors κ, λ', ρ, v, and D_c in Equation (6-11)):

Chapter 7 Numerical results

- Access factor, which depends on the traveller's weight for access time, the routing pattern around the stop, the distribution of the demand around the stop, and which is inversely proportional to access speed;
- Stop loss factor, which is equivalent to the time lost per stop;
- Costs factor, depending on the ratio between operational costs, that is the frequency and the operational costs per vehicle, and traveller costs, patronage and traveller's value of time;
- Maximum speed for public transport;
- Travel distance.

Generally spoken, the values for the optimal stop spacing and line spacing are proportional to these key input factors. Exceptions are the access factor for both stop spacing and line spacing, and maximum speed for line spacing only. Thus a larger stop loss factor implies larger values for stop and line spacing, and a higher weight for access time will lead to lower values for the optimal stop and line spacing.

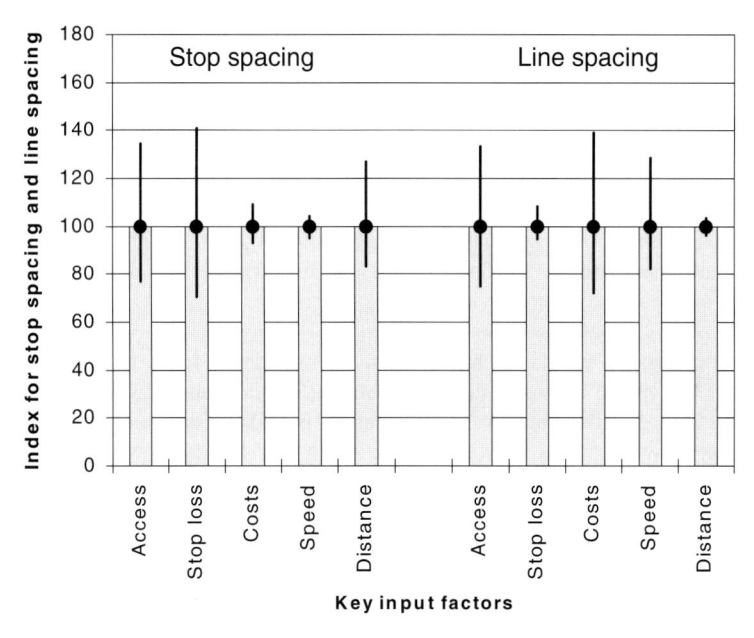

Figure 7-6: Impact on optimal values for stop spacing and line spacing of doubling and halving key input factors for objective function O6.2

Figure 7-6 shows the impact on the optimal values for stop spacing and line spacing for objective function O6 in the cases that these key input factors are doubled or halved. Given the square root relationships found for the optimal stop spacing and line spacing the maximum impact would be an increase of the optimal values of 41 % or a decrease of 29 %. For some key input factors, however, the relationships are not purely proportional, and, furthermore, the optimal stop spacing influences the optimal line spacing and vice versa. As a result, the actual impact of doubling or halving the key input variables will vary between these two extremes.

It is interesting to notice that the costs factor and the maximum speed have no substantial influence on the optimal stop spacing, and that stop loss and travel distance do not affect line spacing. Since the access factor influences both stop spacing and line spacing, it is clearly the most important input factor.

The parameters used in the analysis for the access factor can be considered to be rather conservative. Realistic changes of these assumptions, such as the case of routing patterns directed to and from stops, and in the case of higher densities around stops, will lead to a decrease of the access factor, which results in larger values for the optimal stop and line spacing.

The stop loss factor, that is the time needed for decelerating, alighting and boarding, and accelerating, affects the optimal stop spacing only. The value used, 34 seconds is based on acceleration and deceleration of 1 m/s^2, and a stopping time of 20 seconds. These assumptions appear to be realistic, and certainly no substantial changes are expected

The costs factor is probably the input factor that is most likely to be subjected to discussion. The components for the operational cost are on the safe side, that is, from the operator's point of view. The assumptions for the traveller, on the other hand, are based on an average peak hour. The combination of lower operational costs and higher patronage, however, will clearly lead to adjustments in the costs factor and therefore to shorter line spacing. Lower assumptions for the patronage, on the other hand, will result in significantly larger values for line spacing, and for other periods of the day substantial reductions in patronage are clearly realistic.

The maximum speed that is assumed might be considered to be to optimistic. It will depend on the type of infrastructure available for public transport, and on the priority scheme at traffic signals, whether this assumption is realistic or not. If it is expected that due to delays resulting from other traffic the maximum speed is lower, the stop spacing will not change much, and the optimal line spacing will increase.

The average trip length is clearly an arbitrary assumption. However, it is not unreasonable to assume that the variations will be limited to plus or minus 1 kilometre.

Overall it may be concluded that the results for objective function O6 that are presented in this chapter are quite robust. Changes in assumptions might lead to larger, especially for the access factor, or, in the case of the costs factor, to shorter stop and line spacing. Changes for the other input factors will probably have a limited influence.

7.4.2 Sensitivity for other objective functions

For the other objective functions there are some new input factors that affect the sensitivity of the results presented in the previous sections. Typical examples are:

- Waiting time factor (τ), for objective function O2, minimisation of weighted travel time given an operational budget;
- Fare (r_t) for the objective functions O4, maximising profit, and O5, maximising social welfare;
- Logit coefficient (α) for the relationship between supply and demand for, again, the objective functions O4 and O5.

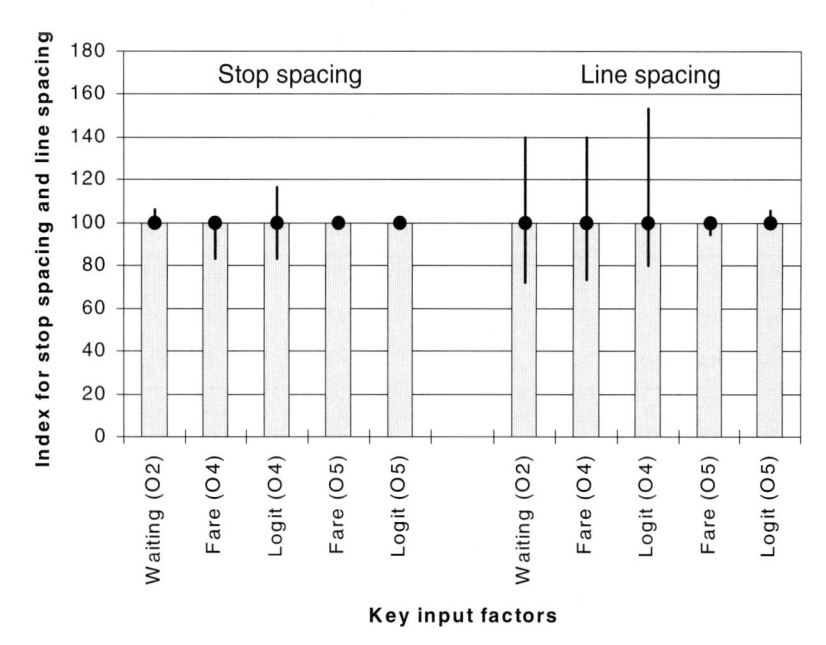

Figure 7-7: Impact on optimal values for stop spacing and line spacing of doubling and halving key input factors for different objective functions

Figure 7-7 shows the sensitivity of the optimal stop and line spacing for changes in these input factors. It presents two striking results. First, stop spacing remains more or less constant. Only changes in the logit-coefficient leads to small changes: an increase of the coefficient, that is a stronger relationship between supply and demand results in slightly shorter stop spacing. Line spacing is clearly more sensitive for these input factors, especially for the objectives O2 and O4.

Second, the optimal stop and line spacing for the objective function social welfare (O5) are not sensitive for changes in these input factors, while the value of the objective function, of course, changes substantially. Since the share of the fare in social welfare is small compared to that of travel time, the limited sensitivity for fare is to be expected. The impact of the logit-coefficient is, at least at first sight, more surprising. It should be noted, however, that in the case of changes in the logit-coefficient the maximum value for travel time used to estimate the consumer surplus (T_c) changes too. The relative changes between two weighted travel times, on the other hand, will still be in same order of size. As a result only the absolute values changes and not the location of the optimum.

The parameters used in the waiting factor are representative for urban public transport networks, having frequencies between 4 and 12 vehicles per hour.

The fare level that is assumed is in fact low, since only the traveller's share is included. An interesting additional sensitivity analysis is, therefore, the case of profit maximisation (O4) while assuming that the current subsidy is included in the fare, that is, the fare is tripled. The results are shown in Table 7-4. It clearly shows that even in the situation where all possible revenues are considered, profit maximisation still results in very coarse networks.

Table 7-4: Sensitivity analysis for the fare level in the case of profit maximisation (O4)

	Bus		Tram	
	Stop spacing	Line spacing	Stop spacing	Line spacing
Traditional	350	500	400	1,000
O4: Subsidy excluded	1,000	2,600	1,200	3,000
O4: Subsidy included	800	1,600	1,000	1,800

Finally, the logit-coefficient used in the analyses is certainly not underestimated. Practical experience has often shown that the demand for public transport can be considered to be a captive market, that is, that the dependency on the quality of the services offered is limited.

7.4.3 Sensitivity for the relationship between supply and demand

The other models for determining the level of demand, that is logit-elasticity and travel-time-ratio, are more sensitive to changes in service level (see also Figure 6-9 up to Figure 6-11). Generally, this larger sensitivity leads to lower values for the optimal stop and line spacing, as can be seen in Table 7-5.

The use of the logit-elasticity results in lower values for both objective functions: profit maximisation (O4), and maximising social welfare (O5).

The use of the travel-time-ratio leads to ambiguous results. In the case of profit maximisation, the values for the optimal stop and line spacing are reduced, as expected. In the case of maximising social welfare (O5), however, the values for the optimal stop and line spacing increase. These higher values are due to the fact that in this case no

Chapter 7 Numerical results 65

weights are applied to the various time elements. As a result the travel times used in the calculation of the consumer surplus are reduced, and thus the consumer surplus is reduced to. As a result the ratio between consumer surplus and operator surplus is changed in favour of the operator, leading to coarser network structures.

Table 7-5: Impact of different travel demand functions on optimal stop and line spacing

	Bus		Tram	
	Stop spacing	Line spacing	Stop spacing	Line spacing
Traditional	350	500	400	1,000
O4: Max. Profit				
Logit-mode-choice	1,000	2,600	1,200	3,000
Logit-elasticity	950	2,100	1,000	2,100
Travel-time-ratio	1,000	1,700	1,200	2,300
O5: Max. Social welfare				
Logit-mode-choice	600	700	800	900
Logit-elasticity	600	500	700	700
Travel-time-ratio	800	800	1,000	1,000

Finally, as stated before (Section 6.6.2), both descriptions do not lead to an optimum for objective O6.1, minimising total costs, even though the shape of the objective function remains shallow. The reduction in patronage more than compensates the increase in travel time, leading to a continuous reduction of the total costs.

7.5 Conclusions

This chapter has shown that in searching for the best public transport network design, a number of relevant and plausible, but essentially different objectives can be adopted. It is shown that the choice of objective clearly matters.

Depending on the objectives, significant differences in network design emerge which result in large differences in performance characteristics. The analyses of both network types show clearly that the traditional network structure in the Netherlands can be improved significantly with regard to operational costs while maintaining or even reducing travel times (and thus having the same patronage).

In the case that line spacing is assumed to be fixed, the simple objective of minimising travel time, already leads to better network characteristics.

Profit maximisation only (O4) leads to profitable but from the traveller's point of view unattractive network structures. The difference in network structures between profit maximisation and for instance maximisation of social welfare is larger than found by Kocur & Hendrickson (1982). In their study, however, fare was a decision variable too, and in their case-study profit maximisation resulted mainly in a significant increase in fare.

Maximising social welfare (O5) proved to be a useful objective. The resulting networks are nearly as attractive or even more attractive than the traditional network structures while the operational costs are significantly less (45 % for the bus network and 15 % for the tram network). Furthermore, this objective is not sensitive for the way the relationship between public transport supply and level of demand is modelled. It is interesting to notice that in the case of the tram network this objective yielded nearly identical results as the simpler objective of minimising total costs given a fixed level of demand (O6.2).

Cost minimisation (O6.1) leads to acceptable results. The fact that modelling the travel demand using logit-elasticities or travel-time-ratio's did not result in an optimal stop spacing nor line spacing for this objective, indicates that if travel demand strongly depends on travel times no realistic solutions may be found. Furthermore, cost minimisation may be achieved by reducing patronage. As a result, it may be concluded that O6.2, while assuming that the travel demand is fixed, is more robust.

O2, minimising travel time under a fixed budget, has been shown to offer possibilities to improve the network characteristics with respect to travel times even further, that is for the bus network. A similar result may be achieved by using the combined approach of Section 6.6.3, in which stop spacing, line spacing, and frequency are determined simultaneously.

In general, the introduction of a variable demand level that depends on the service quality offered does not seriously influence the results for stop spacing and line spacing. The introduction of demand modelling in the objective of minimising total costs seems to be relevant from a theoretical point of view mostly.

The sensitivity analysis showed that the numerical findings presented in this chapter are robust, especially where stop spacing is concerned. The assumptions used are realistic and might be considered to be conservative. Realistic adjustments of assumptions with respect to the routing pattern to and from stops, demand density around stops, or the lower demand level in off-peak hours, result in coarser networks. Only in the case of lower operational cost and higher level of demand, the optimal values for stop spacing, and especially line spacing will decrease.

A possible solution for the poor results of objective O4, at least from the traveller's point of view, is to introduce a subsidy per traveller, for instance, by tripling the fare per traveller. This approach, however, results mainly in larger profits and not in network structures comparable to those found using for instance objective O6. Apparently, a lump-sum subsidy to compensate for non-optimal network structures from the operator's point of view, are more suitable for transport policy measures than a subsidy per traveller.

Chapter 8

IMPLICATIONS FOR PLANNING PRACTICE

This chapter focuses on the implications of the numerical results for planning practice. First, the importance of choosing a specific design objective is discussed. Second, a comparison with actual values is made, and the consequences of adopting the optimal values are discussed. Finally, attention is given to the problem of using these optimal values in actual situations, using a design study for a tramline in the city of The Hague in the Netherlands.

8.1 Importance of choosing objectives

Which objective should be used in public transport network design? Clearly, such a choice is a political one, but every choice has its consequences. The results in Chapter 7 showed that a network that is designed from the traveller's viewpoint only, is expensive, and that a network designed from the operator's perspective only, is unattractive for the traveller.

Intuitively, there has to be a compromise that is optimal from the society's point of view. Typical objectives in that case are maximising social welfare and minimising total costs. These objectives are formulated thus, that a balance is found between the interests of the traveller and those of the operator. A third possible objective from the society's point of view, maximising patronage, is shown to be identical to objectives from the traveller's perspective only. Unless, of course, constraints for the operational budget have been defined. The question then, however, is what that constraint should be? A question, that can be answered using the other two objectives.

The impact of the results found for all these objectives can be illustrated by Figure 8-1 and Figure 8-2. These figures show the relationship between operational costs and (weighted) travel times based on optima found using the various objectives.

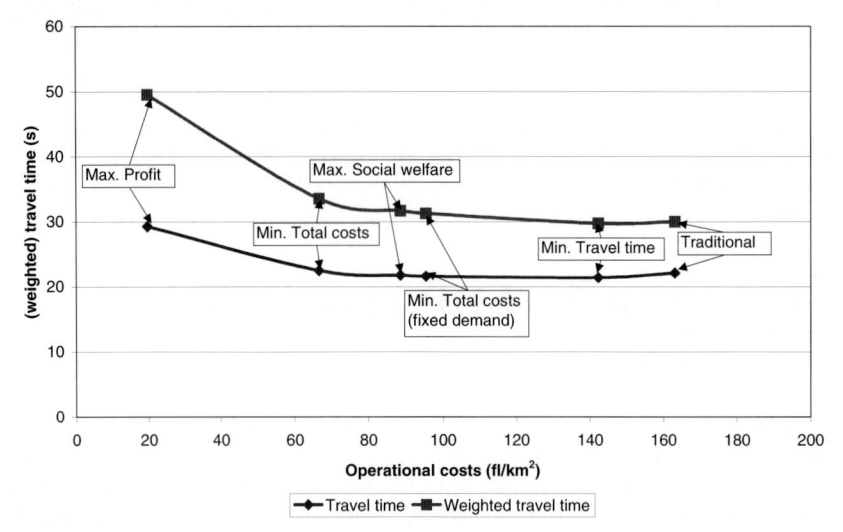

Figure 8-1: Relationship between operational costs and (weighted) travel times for optimised bus networks

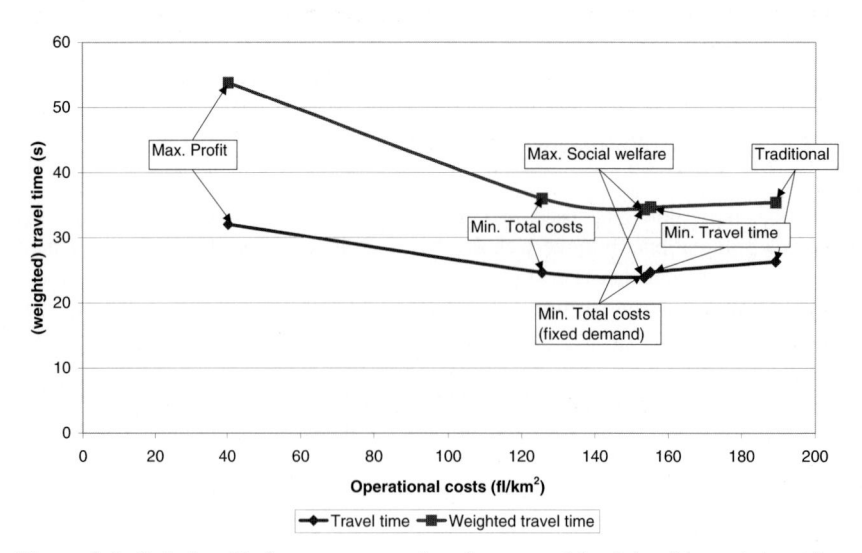

Figure 8-2: Relationship between operational costs and (weighted) travel times for optimised tram networks

Chapter 8 Implications for planning practice

This clearly illustrates that very significant reductions in operational costs are possible without increasing either weighted or unweighted travel times. It is interesting to notice that, if the case of tram networks is compared to that of bus networks, the gap between optimal network structures and traditional design is smaller, and that the gap between operator's perspective and authority's perspective is larger.

A typical finding in Chapter 7 is that for all objectives analysed stop spacing should be increased, and for bus networks line spacing too. Which objective then was used for the existing public transport networks? One assumption is that what seemed to be good planning practice prevailed in network design, even though the characteristics of the design problem changed over time, especially the size of the cities. This assumption is supported by the fact that the current values for stop spacing can be replicated if the design is focused on short trips, that is 2 kilometres for bus networks and 3 kilometres for tram networks, and if the simple objective of minimising travel time (O1) is used. Using the more preferred objective of minimising total costs (O6.2), however, will still result in significantly higher values.

A second assumption might be that the current design is focused on accessibility only, for instance, by defining maximum walking distances. The main argument is then that travellers are not willing to walk more than 400 metres to a stop. This is often supported by research done by Walther (1973). Walther found that in Bielefeld the demand for public transport decreases as the access distance increases, and drops to nil if the access distance is larger than 400 up to 600 metres. This causal relationship, however, is questionable. Do people really have a maximum access distance or is it just so that in Bielefeld the public network characteristics are such that it is not necessary to walk more than 400 metres? In the latter case, the maximum access distance is not a result of the analysis but it was already, although implicitly, an input-factor in the analysis. In this context it is interesting to notice that using traveller oriented objectives, in which explicitly is accounted for the travellers weights for the various time elements, network structures were found having shorter weighted door-to-door travel times. Apparently the focus on accessibility already leads to sub-optimal travel times: the access time is short but the in-vehicle time is long because the bus has to stop too often.

For both assumptions, that is, shorter travel distances or the focus on accessibility, it is questionable whether they are still applicable. Cities have grown significantly and the evidence for a maximum access distance is limited. Furthermore, it is widely recognised that the cost efficiency of public transport should be improved. Maintaining these old design principles leads certainly to expensive network structures.

The alternative is to use objectives in public transport network design that combine the viewpoints of the traveller and the operator, such as maximising social welfare or minimising total costs. In both objectives, the benefits for the user as well as the benefits for the operator are accounted for. Furthermore, for the cities of today a choice must be made for which trip types a public transport network is designed: short trips for which walking and cycling are interesting alternatives, or for longer trips from the outer areas to the city centre?

Opting for these more realistic objectives and for these trip types will result in better network structures. They are more attractive for the traveller because, although access distance increases the in-vehicle time decreases, and in the case of bus networks waiting time decreases too, leading to shorter door-to-door travel times. And these network structures are interesting as the operational costs are reduced significantly. Increasing stop spacing only leads to a cost reduction of 15 % up to 20 %. If, as in the case of the bus network, line spacing increases too, the reduction of operational costs increases up to 40 %.

Finally, in the context of the current more market oriented approach of public transport, it is interesting to notice that profit maximisation alone does not necessarily result in attractive public transport networks, even not in the case that the current subsidy is included in the revenues. A better approach might be to define the main characteristics such as stop and line spacing, and the expected level of patronage beforehand, for instance using the objective of maximising social welfare, and then put the actual operation of the transport services out to tender to minimise the deficit. It might be interesting for the operator to increase the patronage, for instance by offering additional services or by using specific marketing strategies, if he receives (part of) the additional revenues. In this case the optimal network structure from a social point of view is guaranteed, while there are enough possibilities for the operator to improve his economical results.

8.2 Adopting larger stop and line spacing

A clear conclusion from the analyses for both network types is that stop spacing as it is traditionally applied in urban public transport networks should be increased significantly, irrespective of the particular objective that is used. For cities having a bus network an average stop spacing of 600 to 700 metres would be more appropriate, while for tram systems the average stop spacing should be about 800 metres.

The impact of these recommendations on the network structure is illustrated in Figure 8-3. It is interesting to notice that there is not much difference between the optimal network characteristics of a bus network or a tram network. Apparently, a tram network is equivalent to a bus network having only higher demand and higher trip lengths, which compensate the higher operational costs.

Table 1-1 showed actual values for stop spacing for urban public transport networks in the Netherlands that range between 350 and 450 metres. These values are in accordance to the values presented for the traditional network structures. Furthermore, these values are not limited to the Dutch context. The network in Zurich has a stop spacing of 400 metres (Schäffeler, 1999) while for American cities stop spacing values ranging between 200 and 400 metres have been reported (Furth & Rahbee, 2000). It is therefore concluded that the recommendation that stop spacing should be increased not only applies to the situation in the Netherlands.

Chapter 8 Implications for planning practice

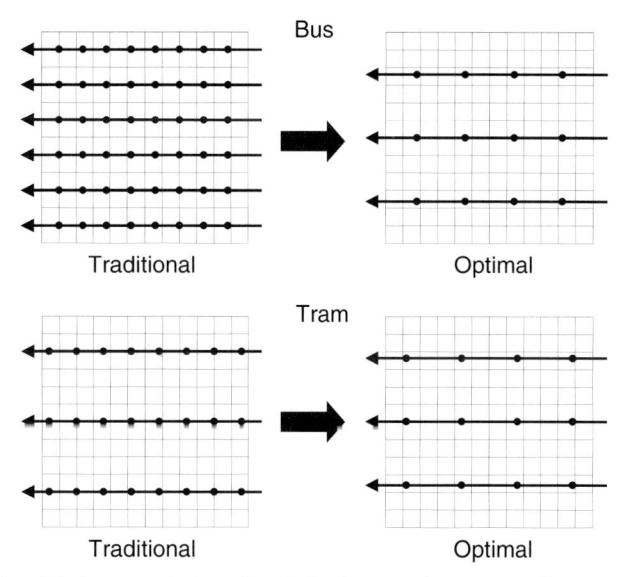

Figure 8-3: Spatial characteristics of optimised networks compared to traditional design

In the Netherlands, however, there is a typical exception, that is the city of Almere. This new town was designed to be served by a public transport system having dedicated buslanes. The average stop spacing in this city is 600 metres and the line spacing is about 800 metres (De Heij & Maassen (1995)). These values are clearly in line with the results presented here. As a result it has the highest cost efficiency ratio of all urban public transport systems in the Netherlands.

The conclusion that stop spacing should be increased also supports new developments in urban public transport planning such as Tram Plus in the city of Rotterdam (Projectbureau Tram Plus (1994)), and AggloNet in the agglomeration of the city of The Hague (Stadsgewest Haaglanden (1999)). The increase in stop spacing that is proposed in these concepts, however, is still small compared to the optimal values found in this report. For Tram Plus a stop spacing of 500 metres is proposed and for AggloNet a stop spacing of 600 metres. The latter seems to more in line with the recommendations presented here than Tram Plus, but given the scale of the network of AggloNet the average trip length will be larger, leading to higher optimal values than 800 metres. As a result the stop spacing for AggloNet might still be too small.

Finally, it is interesting to notice that these results are in line with the results presented by Egeter (1993). Egeter studied numerous combinations of design variables with respect to the average travel time and concluded that a stop spacing of 600 metres would be best. His approach can be described as adopting objective O2, that is minimising travel time on a fixed budget. A limitation of the analysis by Egeter is that only a limited set of values for the stop spacing was taken into account: 300, 600 and 1.200 metres. The findings presented in Chapter 7 show that given these three values for the stop spacing only, 600 metres is indeed the best. However, although these results were even included in official guidelines for public transport planning (Projectbureau IVVS (1995)), current stop spacing is still too small. Apparently, public companies are conservative with respect to their network concepts.

8.3 Case studies

Another argument for maintaining the current values for stop spacing and line spacing might be that the actual situational context, for instance road network characteristics and the location of urban facilities, does not allow for larger values. Intuitively there might be some truth in this. However, it should be noticed that the values for stop spacing and line spacing found in Chapter 7, are average values, and that Chapter 6 showed that the objective functions are shallow or flat around the optimum, which allows for adjustments because of specific local situations. This implies that using some creativity, the larger values for stop spacing and line spacing should applicable in reality too, unless there are constraints in the actual planning of stops that limit the range for the average stop spacing and line spacing. A clear example of such a constraint is the road spacing in an urban area. Given the road spacing, the line spacing should be a multiple of it. The optimal value for line spacing in a tram network might therefore not be applicable in reality. The recommendations for the bus network, however, shows that the line spacing should be nearly twice as large as in traditional networks, which may be very realistic indeed.

Koot & Govers (1995) applied the guidelines defined by Egeter (1993) to three cities in the Netherlands: Dordrecht, Tilburg and The Hague. Two cases were considered: an urban network having a stop spacing of 600 metres, and a two-level network consisting of a traditional urban public transport network and a higher level network having a stop spacing of 1.000 metres. For Dordrecht is was found that the directness of the routes could be improved significantly. Only in the more historical neighbourhoods, the road network proved to be an important constraint. Apparently, there were no problems in applying a stop spacing of 600 metres. The cost reduction ranged between 10 % up to 30 %. In the case of Tilburg an assessment was made of the impact on travel demand. As expected, it was found that the demand dropped close to the city centre and increased as the travel distance increased. The net effect was an increase of 7 %, while the operational costs were reduced by 10 % to 15 %. The Hague proved to be the only city for which a two level network structure might be suitable. The travel distances in the other two cities were to short. The net effect on the operational costs, however, was limited to 5 %. From these analyses it can be concluded that an average stop spacing of 600 metres must be possible in practice.

Another application of the concepts defined by Egeter (1993) can be found in Roedoe (1995). In his study Roedoe applied these concepts to the city of Haarlem in the Netherlands, with the assumption of a fixed operational budget. He concluded that the stop spacing should be doubled to 700 metres, leading to an increase of 10 % of the kilometres travelled. A more detailed application for the neighbourhood of Schalkwijk showed that due to local constraints in that case the maximum possible stop spacing is 590 metres.

Chapter 8 Implications for planning practice   73

Schäffeler (1999) made a detailed study of the possibilities for changing the stop spacing for the case of specific tramline: line 2 in the city of The Hague. This tramline is located in the southern part of The Hague and offers a direct route to the city centre and the main railway station in The Hague. The total line length is 7.4 kilometres and the line has 21 stops, leading to an average stop spacing of 370 metres. Figure 8-4 gives an overview of the stops, the stop spacing and the transfer possibilities of tramline 2. In the future, a tram tunnel will replace the part in the city centre, the grey coloured area.

It is clear that this stop spacing of 370 metres is clearly too small compared to the results derived in the previous chapter. Based on these results, the optimal stop spacing should range between 600 and 800 metres. Schäffeler found that the current average trip length was 4 kilometres, which would allow for slightly shorter stop spacing. However, the average trip length would increase if short trips, for instance, to and from transfer nodes or local shopping centres were excluded.

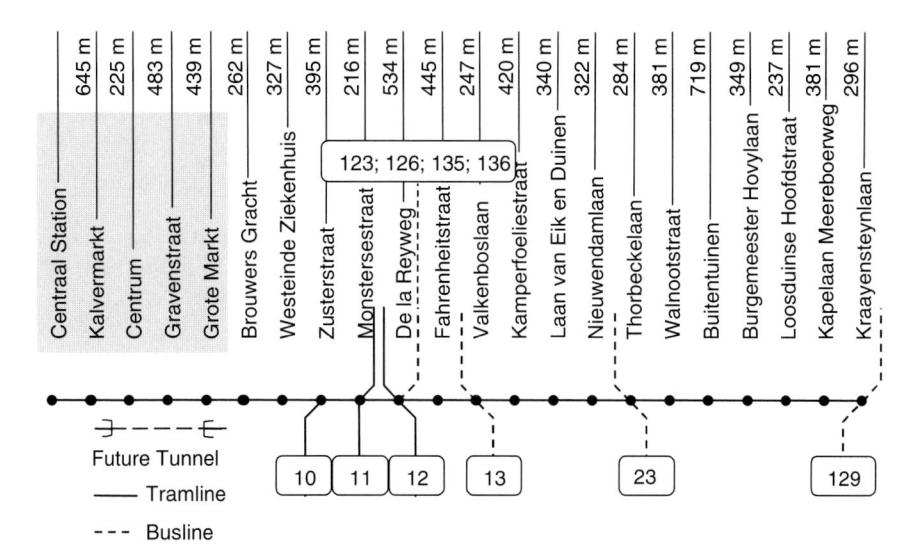

Figure 8-4: Lay out of stops for tramline 2, including transfer nodes and stop spacing

In his analysis he first made a list of all possible stop locations along the line. Second, he defined four criteria to assess the importance of each location:

1. Characteristics of access routes;
2. Location of main roads that have to be crossed;
3. Demand density and location of important facilities, such as hospitals;
4. Transfer possibilities to perpendicular lines.

This analysis showed that from the 20 possible stop locations outside the city centre 7 stop locations had a low, and 3 locations had a high potential. Using this assessment of the possible locations Schäffeler tried to allocate stops for tramline 2 using four values for the average stop spacing: 450 metres, 600 metres, 750 metres, and 1,000 metres. The results of this analysis are shown in Figure 8-5.

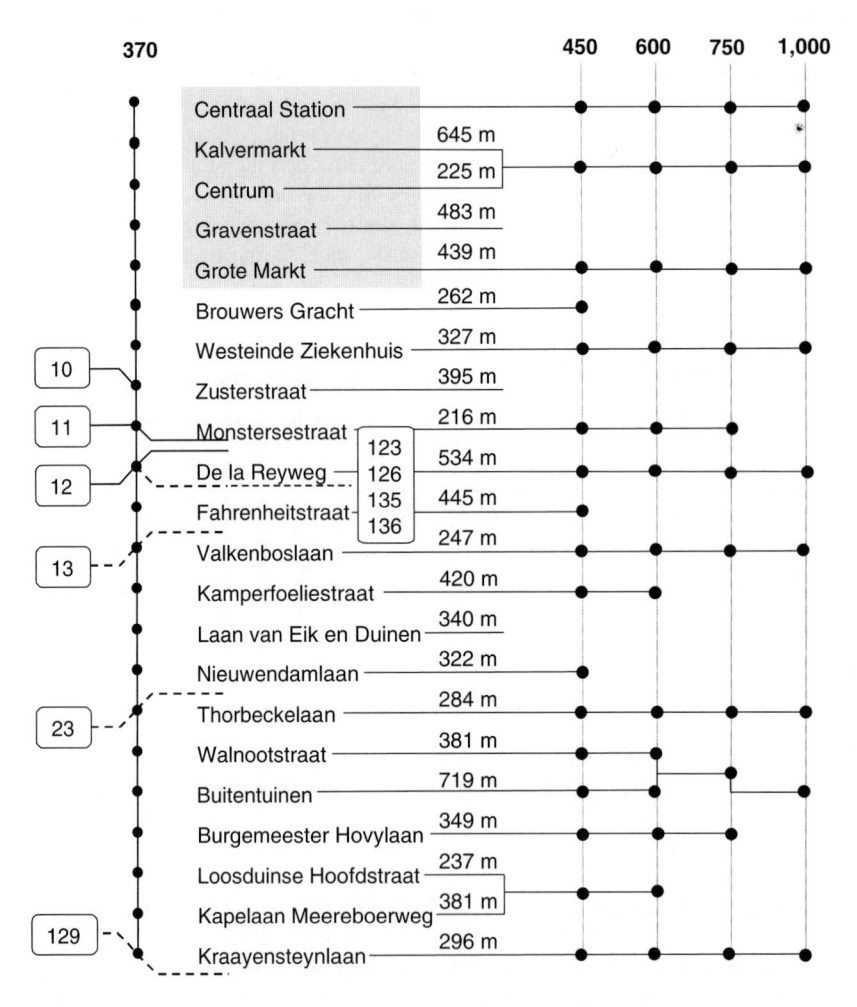

Figure 8-5: Results of allocating stops for four scenarios for the average stop spacing of respectively 400, 600, 750, and 1,000 metres

Schäffeler had no problems in allocating stops at an average value of 450 metres. Two stops were dropped and two stops were replaced by a new stop. The eliminated stops were selected because of their closeness to an adjacent stop or their limited potential. The resulting stop spacing is 460 metres.

Chapter 8 Implications for planning practice

The scenario of an average stop spacing of 600 metres did not lead to any major difficulties too. Three additional stops were skipped, which resulted in an average stop spacing of 570 metres. Since two adjacent stops were skipped there is a part of the line having a stop spacing of more than 1,000 metres. This is not a problem, however, since the line passes a cemetery and at this location there is a parallel tramline at a distance of 500 metres.

The third scenario, that is 750 metres, provided more difficulties. Dropping another two stops stretched the stretch passing the cemetery further, and a new stop replaced two other stops.

The fourth scenario of an average stop spacing of 1,000 metres, made it necessary to drop a transfer node and to drop additional stops at the end of the line.

Each scenario was evaluated for travel time and operational costs. The results are shown in Table 8-1.

Table 8-1: Evaluation of four scenarios for the stop spacing of tramline 2 (Schäffeler, 1999)

Scenario	Average stop spacing (m)	Door-to-door travel time (min)	Operational costs (fl/km^2)
Reference	370	21.8	64
450	460	21.4	59
600	570	21.1	54
750	740	21.3	49
1,000	930	22.1	45

From this evaluation Schäffeler concluded that a stop spacing of 600 metres is optimal. It results in the shortest travel time, the operational costs are reduced by 15 %, and the urban characteristics were no significant constraint in allocating stops. From these results, however, it might also be concluded that a stop spacing of 750 metres would be best. The travel time is still lower than today, while the operational costs are decreased further to 77 %. Of course, there remains the fact that in this case it proved to be more difficult to allocate the stops in a regular pattern. The resulting stop pattern seems therefore somewhat artificial. The conclusion from this analysis is that the urban characteristics limit the average stop spacing to 600 metres preferably and to a maximum of 750 metres at most.

Chapter 9

FURTHER ANALYSES USING ANALYTICAL MODELS

In the previous chapters the analytical models were used for a specific situation: an urban corridor in which the public transport network offers services to the city centre. A typical characteristic of an analytical model, however, is that it can easily be used for other types of analysis. An analytical model, for instance, can be extended to other line types, or might be used to investigate the implications of new ideas for network design. In this chapter the following topics will be discussed:

- Extension from an urban corridor to a network;
- Extension from a peak hour to daily operations;
- Optimal stop spacing in city centres;
- Influence of specific traveller groups on network design;
- Impact of a multimodal approach, that is, the impact of cycling as an access mode.

9.1 Extension to a network

Since urban public transport systems play an important role in the accessibility of city centres, the focus on trips to the city centre is certainly justified. There are, however, other trip types for which an urban public transport network might be used, for instance, trips coming from the city centre, transversal trips with or without transfers, and tangential trips. The characteristics of each trip type will be different from those used in the previous chapters, and as a result the optimal values for stop spacing and line spacing will be different too. The question then is whether considering these other trip types will have a significant influence on the results presented in this report.

9.1.1 Conceptual approach

The different trip types determine the formulation of the weighted travel time, which is used in the various objectives. The building blocks presented in Chapter 4 can easily be used to formulate the weighted travel time for other trip types (Figure 9-1).

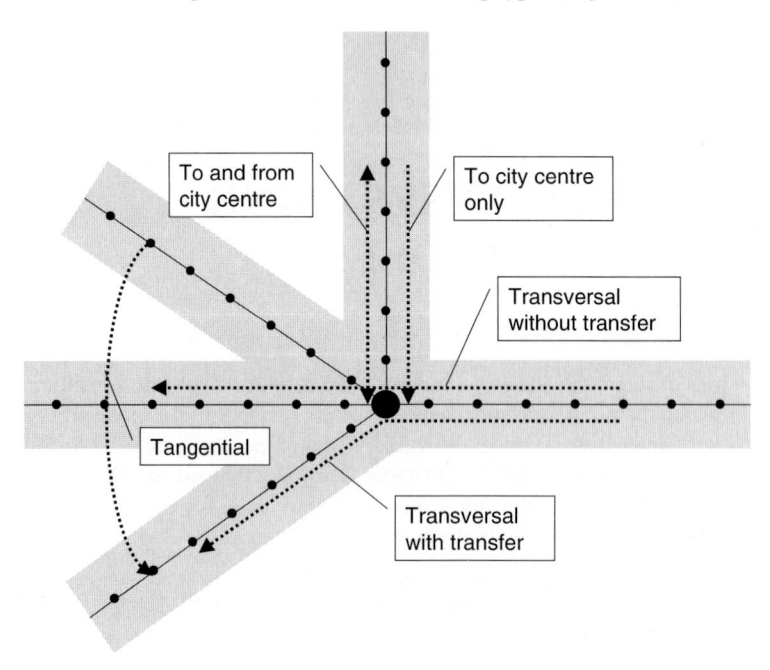

Figure 9-1: Different trip types in a network consisting of urban corridors

In the case of trips coming from the city centre, the access time within the city centre can be considered to be fixed, and the building block for the access time can be used to describe the egress time outside the city centre. Since the weight for egress time is smaller than that for access time, the optimal values for stop and line spacing will increase. In the case of transversal trips the stop and line spacing influence both access time as well as egress time. At the same time the average trip length increases. The overall effect is a small decrease of stop and line spacing. In the case that a transversal trip requires a transfer, however, the waiting time occurs twice: at the first stop and at the transfer. This results, again, in larger values for stop and line spacing. The tentative conclusion from this conceptual analysis is, that in the case of centre oriented lines, accounting for other trips types will sooner lead to larger values than to smaller values. For tangential lines, however, smaller values are possible, since stop and line spacing influences access time as well as egress time, while the average trip length is likely to be reduced.

9.1.2 Formalisation

This line of reasoning can be formalised, using the objective of minimisation of total costs given a fixed level of demand (O6.2). The objective function can be written as:

$$\left\{ w_a \cdot T_a + w_w \cdot T_w + \frac{D_c}{D_s} \cdot \left(\frac{D_s}{v} + T_s \right) + w_e \cdot T_e \right\} \cdot P \cdot c_t + C_o \tag{9-1}$$

The demand for public transport P can be divided into different trip types P_j, each of them having its own trip characteristics. These typical characteristics can be denoted by the variables y_{xj}, which represent the relative change in the weights for trip time element x and travel distances used in the analysis of an urban corridor only. For trips to the city centre, for instance, y_e will be zero because in this case the egress time is assumed to be fixed. The total costs can then be defined as the weighted sum of the travel times for each sub-population:

$$\sum_j \left\{ \begin{array}{l} w_a \cdot y_{aj} \cdot P_j \cdot T_a + w_w \cdot y_{wj} \cdot P_j \cdot T_w + \\ y_{cj} \cdot D_c \cdot P_j \cdot \left(\frac{1}{v} + \frac{T_s}{D_s} \right) + w_e \cdot y_{ej} \cdot P_j \cdot T_e \end{array} \right\} \cdot c_t + C_o \tag{9-2}$$

where:

y_{xj} = multiplier for trip time element x and trip type j

P_j = number of trips for trip type j

Due to the additive nature of the equation and to the fact that the building blocks itself are independent on the trip type, Equation (9-2) can be rewritten as:

$$\left[\begin{array}{l} \sum_j (w_a \cdot y_{aj} \cdot P_j) \cdot T_a + \sum_j (w_w \cdot y_{wj} \cdot P_j) \cdot T_w + \\ \sum_j (y_{cj} \cdot D_c \cdot P_j) \cdot \left(\frac{1}{v} + \frac{T_s}{D_s} \right) + \sum_j (w_e \cdot y_{ej} \cdot P_j) \cdot T_e \end{array} \right] \cdot c_t + C_o \tag{9-3}$$

This equation can be simplified to an equation that is similar to Equation (9-1):

$$\left\{ \overline{w}_a \cdot T_a + \overline{w}_w \cdot T_w + \frac{\overline{D}_c}{D_s} \cdot \left(\frac{D_s}{v} + T_s \right) + \overline{w}_e \cdot T_e \right\} \cdot P \cdot c_t + C_o \tag{9-4}$$

where:

$$\overline{w}_x = \frac{\sum_j (w_x \cdot y_{xj} \cdot P_j)}{P} \quad \text{for time element } x$$

$$\overline{D}_c = \frac{\sum_j (y_{xj} \cdot D_c \cdot P_j)}{P}$$

Since T_e depends on D_s and D_l, building block BB2 for T_a can be used to define T_e too, lading to the final formulation of the objective function.

$$\left\{(\overline{w}_a + \overline{w}_e) \cdot T_a + \overline{w}_w \cdot T_w + \frac{\overline{D}_c}{D_s} \cdot \left(\frac{D_s}{v} + T_s\right)\right\} \cdot P \cdot c_t + C_o \qquad (9\text{-}5)$$

This objective function can for instance be used for the case of the bus network in which different combinations of trip types are considered:

- Trips to the city centre only, that is the case studied in Section 7.2;
- Trips to and from the city centre;
- 25 % of transversal trips, of which $^2/_3$ has a transfer in the city centre;
- 33 % of transversal trips, of which $^3/_5$ has a transfer;
- 50% of transversal trips, of which ½ has a transfer.

The impact of these combinations of trip types of the overall weights in Equation (9-5) is shown in Table 9-1. If these overall weights are compared to those for the simple case of trips to the city centre only, it is clear that in general the weight for waiting time as well as the average trip length have a larger increase than the weight for access time.

Table 9-1: Overall weights for different combinations of trip types

	To city centre only	To and from city centre	25 % transversal	33 % transversal	50 % transversal
Overall weight for access time	2.2	1.7	2.0	2.2	2.5
Overall weight for waiting time	1.5	1.5	1.7	1.8	1.9
Overall trip length	3.0	3.0	3.7	4.0	4.5

Since waiting time plays an important role for transversal trips, frequency should be included as a decision variable too, or the stepwise procedure used in Chapter 7 should be applied. In this case the objective function of Equation (9-5) is optimised for all three variables simultaneously (see Section 6.6.3). In this way it is always guaranteed that the operational costs balance the traveller's costs. The results are shown in Figure 9-2. Stop spacing increases in all cases, and there is only a slight decrease of the line spacing in the last case: 50 % transversal trips. The results presented in the previous chapters are therefore robust. Inclusion of other trip types will certainly not lead to shorter values for stop and line spacing.

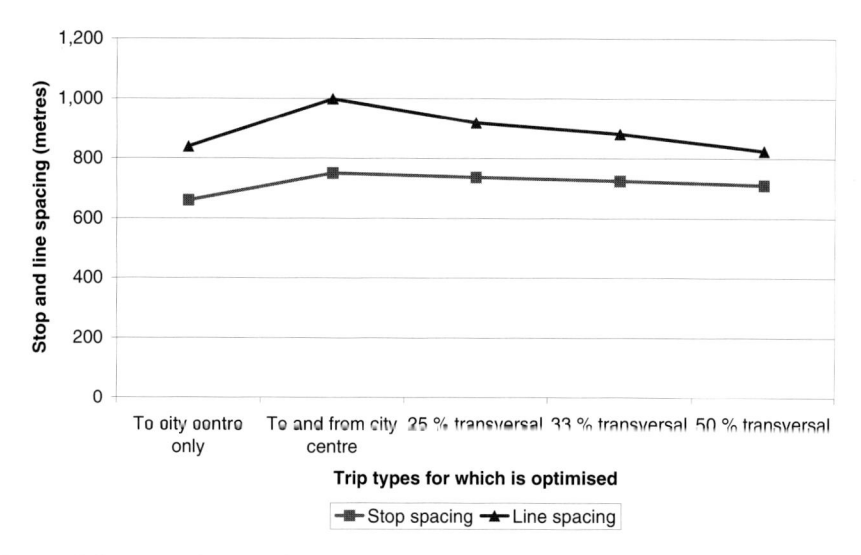

Chapter 9 Further analyses using analytical models 81

Figure 9-2: Optimal values for stop and line spacing for different combinations of trip types (O6.2)

9.1.3 Radial network

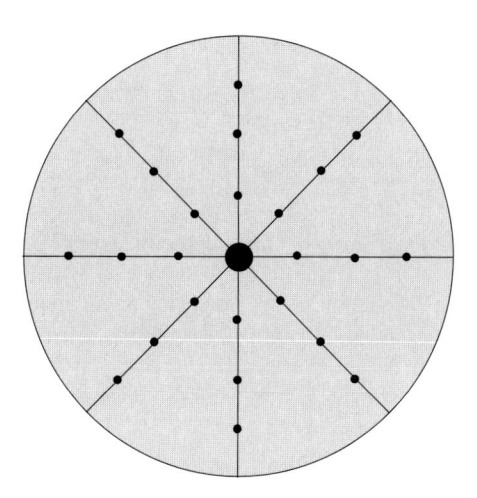

Figure 9-3: Lay out of a radial network

Similar results can be found if, instead of an urban corridor, a radial network is studied (Figure 9-3).

In this case objective function O6.2, minimisation of the total costs given a fixed level of demand, changes for the following aspects (see also Figure 9-4):
- The objective function is defined for the whole city instead of for a part of one square kilometre;
- The decision variable line spacing is replaced by the number of radial lines N_r;
- Access distance is split up in a part parallel to the line, which depends on stop spacing only, and a part perpendicular to the line, depending on the number of radial lines;
- Within a radial network two trip types must be taken into account: radial trips and transversal trips. As a result the weight factors for access time, waiting time, egress time, and the average trip length too, must be weighed by the share of both trip types.

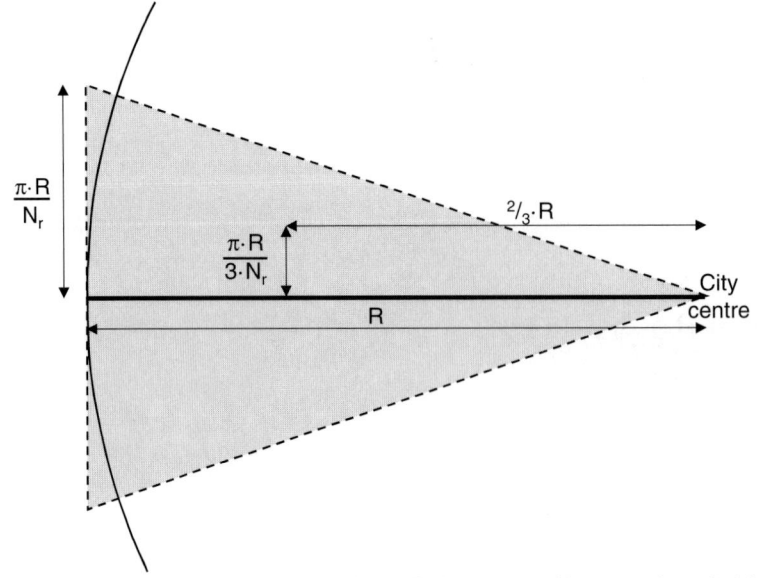

Figure 9-4: Lay out for a segment of a radial city served by a single radial line

The operational costs are a function of the frequency F, the number of radials N_r and of the total in-vehicle time per radial line in two directions:

$$C_o = F \cdot N_r \cdot \frac{2 \cdot R}{D_s} \cdot \left(\frac{D_s}{v} + T_s \right) \cdot c_o \qquad (9\text{-}6)$$

The travel time is weighted for the different trip types included in the analysis, which leads to the following formulation of the objective function:

$$\left\{ (\overline{w}_a + \overline{w}_e) \cdot \left(\frac{f_a \cdot D_s}{v_a} + \frac{f_c \cdot R}{v_a \cdot N_r} \right) + \overline{w}_w \cdot \frac{f_w}{F} + \frac{\overline{D}_c}{D_s} \cdot \left(\frac{D_s}{v} + T_s \right) + \overline{T}_{et} \right\} \cdot P \cdot c_t + C_o \qquad (9\text{-}7)$$

Chapter 9 Further analyses using analytical models

where:

f_c = factor for access distance perpendicular to the line : $\dfrac{\pi}{3}$

$\overline{T}_{et}$ = constant for egress time of city oriented trips and transferpenalty for transversal trips

Simultaneous optimisation for all three decision variables yields the following set of equations:

$$D_s^{*2} = \frac{\lambda'}{\kappa' \cdot f_a} \cdot \left(\rho' \cdot F^* \cdot N_r^* + \overline{D}_c \right) \qquad (9\text{-}8a)$$

$$N_r^{*2} = \frac{\kappa' \cdot f_c \cdot R}{\lambda} \cdot \left(\frac{1}{\dfrac{\rho'}{D_s^*} + \dfrac{\rho'}{\lambda' \cdot v}} \right) \cdot \frac{1}{F^*} \qquad (9\text{-}8b)$$

$$F^{*2} = \frac{\tau'}{\lambda'} \cdot \left(\frac{1}{\dfrac{\rho'}{D_s^*} + \dfrac{\rho'}{\lambda' \cdot v}} \right) \cdot \frac{1}{N_r^*} \qquad (9\text{-}8c)$$

where:

$\kappa' = \dfrac{w_a}{v_a}$

$\lambda' = T_s$

$\rho' = \dfrac{2 \cdot R \cdot c_o}{P \cdot c_t}$

$\tau' = w_w \cdot f_w$

This model is solved for two cases: a bus network and a tram network. In both cases the parameters specified in Table 7-1 are used. Furthermore the radius of the cities is 4.5 and 7.5 kilometres respectively, yielding average trip lengths to the city centre of 3 and 5 kilometres, which makes the analysis comparable to that in Chapter 7. Finally, it is assumed that all trips are oriented at the city centre, or that only 67 % of the trips are oriented at the city centre.

Table 9-2: Optimal values for frequency, stop and line spacing for an urban corridor and a radial network (O6.2)

	Bus			Tram		
	Corridor	Radial network		Corridor	Radial network	
Percentage centre oriented *(%)*	100	100	67	100	100	67
Stop spacing *(m)*	700	700	700	800	800	800
Line spacing[*] *(m)*	900	900	900	900	1,000	1,000
Stop density *(/km²)*	1.6	1.9	2.0	1.4	1.6	1.6
Line density *(/km²)*	1.1	1.4	1.5	1.1	1.3	1.4
Frequency *(veh/h)*	5.9	5.9	6.8	6.0	5.5	6.4
Number of radials	-	20	21	-	32	32
Weighted travel time to city centre *(min)*	30.2	30.2	29.2	34.4	35.8	34.8
Operational costs *(fl/km²)*	95	126	146	153	170	196

[*] *For the radial city the line spacing is calculated as the average access distance perpendicular to the line divided by the access factor f_a*

The results (see Table 9-2) clearly show that the optimal values for a radial network are nearly identical to those for an urban corridor. In the case that transversal trips are included too, the frequency and therefore the operational costs increase. The difference between the service areas per line type, however, yields different performance characteristics. Compared to the rectangular service area in an urban corridor, the wedge shaped service area in a radial network results in a higher line density and therefore in higher operational costs. It is interesting to notice that in the case of the tram network the weighted travel time to the city centre increases for a radial city. Apparently, the city has become too large to be serviced with a radial network.

9.2 Extension to daily operations

All analyses presented in the previous chapters focus on a typical peak hour. The results for the tram network, for instance, imply that a small profit is possible. Public transport services, however, operate outside these peak hours too. The main difference for the off-peak periods is that demand decreases substantially. A common approach is to change the frequencies for the different periods of the day. The sensitivity analysis on the other hand, showed that a lower level of demand implies a coarser network in order to guarantee adequate frequencies. How then, can the concepts presented in this report be used for networks that have to operate under varying demand levels during the day?

Chapter 9 Further analyses using analytical models

In order to answer this question four strategies are considered:
1. Traditional network structure and varying the frequencies;
2. Optimal network structure for the peak hour and varying the frequencies;
3. Optimal network structure for an average demand level and varying the frequencies;
4. Optimal network structures for each of three typical periods: peak demand, normal demand, and low demand.

The three typical periods (peak, normal, and low demand) are used to calculate the operational costs per period and for an average day. It is assumed that the demand level is halved between peak and normal demand, and between normal and low demand. Since frequencies obviously play an important role in the analysis, the objective function of minimising total costs is solved for all three decision variables simultaneously.

Table 9-3: Results for different strategies for bus network design for daily operations

	Traditional	Optimal peak	Optimal average demand	Optimal per period
Stop spacing *(m)*	350	650	700	650/700/750
Line spacing *(m)*	500	800	1,000	800/1,050/1,350
Frequency by period *(veh/h)*	4/4/2	6/4/2	6/5/2	6/5/4
Average travel time *(min)*	23.3	22.3	22.4	21.2
Average weighted travel time *(min)*	31.8	32.9	33.8	31.9
Daily operator costs *(fl/km²)*	2,446	1,274	1,105	1,265
Cost effectiveness	29%	56%	64%	56%
Total daily trip costs per traveller *(fl)*	7.87	6.83	6.80	6.65

Note: Adopted parameters are given in Table 7-1

In the case of a bus network with average trip distance of 3 kilometres (Table 9-3) it is found that using optimal values for the stop and line spacing accounts for the largest increase of the cost effectiveness compared to the traditional network structure. If an optimal stop and line spacing is used the best result is found in the case that the average demand level is used to determine the optimal network structure. In this case the daily operational costs are the lowest and the cost effectiveness therefore maximal. Focussing on the peak period proves to be expensive. If instead of cost effectiveness, the total daily trip costs per traveller weighted by the demand level are considered, it is preferable to vary the network structure per period. The operational costs are slightly higher, but the average travel times are reduced. This is especially true for the period having a low demand because of the higher frequency in that period.

The results for a tram network having an average trip distance of 5 kilometres (Table 9-4) are similar. The highest cost effectiveness is found if the stop and line spacing are optimised for an average demand level, and the total trip costs per traveller are lowest in the case that each period has it's own network structure. The only difference is that the gap between the traditional network structure and the optimised networks is smaller.

Table 9-4: Results for different strategies for tram network design for daily operations

	Traditional	Optimal peak	Optimal average demand	Optimal per period
Stop spacing *(m)*	400	800	800	800/800/900
Line spacing *(m)*	1,000	900	1,100	900/1,150/1,400
Frequency by period *(veh/h)*	6/4/2	6/4/2	6/5/2	6/5/4
Average travel time *(min)*	28.9	26.5	26.7	25.4
Average weighted travel time *(min)*	39.4	38.3	39.0	37.2
Daily operator costs *(fl/km²)*	2,145	1,739	1,590	1,793
Cost effectiveness	69%	85%	93%	83%
Total daily trip costs per traveller *(fl)*	8.37	7.85	7.84	7.70

Note: Adopted parameter values are given in Table 7-1

It should be noted that for daily operations the cost effectiveness for both the bus network and the tram network are below hundred percent. The maximum cost effectiveness found for the bus network is 64 % and for the tram network 93 %. Additional subsidy will be necessary for urban public transport.

Furthermore, the cost effectiveness on a daily basis for especially the tram network is much higher than is currently found in Dutch cities (see Appendix B). This might be due to higher frequencies in the network of the city of The Hague in the peak period in order to accommodate the demand and/or in the period with a low demand level because of minimum frequencies. Both lines of reasoning might also be applied to the optimised network, which will accordingly reduce the cost effectiveness.

9.3 Stop spacing in city centres

An interesting result derived in earlier research is that, if a variable stop spacing is considered, the stop spacing should increase near the city centre (Black (1978), Spasovic & Schonfeld (1993), Kuah & Perl (1988)). The main explanation for this result is that each stop leads to longer travel times and that therefore the number of stops should be limited, especially for travellers making longer trips. It might be questioned whether this conclusion still holds if city centres are no longer considered being single nodes having fixed egress times.

Let us, for instance, assume that the unit area is located in the city centre and that the stop spacing outside the city centre is fixed. The only decision variable then is the stop spacing within the city centre. For the simple objective O1, access time must be replaced by egress time. For trips in an urban area it has been found that the weight of egress time is half the weight of access time (Van der Waard (1988)). The trip length for which the in-vehicle time is influenced by the stop spacing in the city centre, however, is strongly reduced, for instance 500 up to 1,000 metres. The time lost per stop might be larger because of the larger number of travellers boarding the line, let us say an increase of 50 %. Finally, the stops will be located at locations having higher densities, which will reduce the access distance with for instance a factor ½. Using Equation (6-3), it can be calculated how optimal stop spacing should change. Table 9-5 shows that using these assumptions it is not directly obvious whether the stop spacing within the city centre should increase or not. For the more realistic cases of a small city centre with a bus network, or a large city centre with a tram network, however, the stop spacing should at least remain constant. Only in the case of a small city centre with a tram network a decrease of the stop spacing might be relevant.

Table 9-5: Relative change of the stop spacing within the city centre compared to the stop spacing outside the city centre

Trip length within the city centre	Bus network	Tram network
500 metres	100 %	77 %
1,000 metres	-	110 %

This argumentation only holds if the city centre is the only major destination of the public transport line. In many cities the main public transport lines offer transport to and from the railway station too or are transversal lines. In the case that these lines have to pass the city centre first, the original argument for increasing the stop spacing near the destination, that is avoiding delays for travellers who have to travel further, is still relevant. Therefore, it might be concluded that the stop spacing of urban public transport systems should certainly not decrease near the city centre.

9.4 Influence of opting for specific traveller groups

The generic formulation of the objectives allows analysing what the outcomes would be if, instead of the average traveller, specific groups of travellers would be considered. Different groups of travellers can be characterised by differences in value of time, in sensitivity in mode choice, in trip lengths, and in weight factors for the different time elements. Since the main dilemma for the seven objectives is the dilemma between access time versus in-vehicle time, the effect of different weight factors will be analysed further. For the objectives used, the weight factors for access time and waiting time are relevant.

Van der Waard (1988) established weight factors for different traveller groups, presented in Table 9-6.

Table 9-6: Weights for access time and waiting time for different population groups (Van der Waard 1988)

Population	Access	Waiting
Car available	1.7	1.8
No car available	2.5	1.5
30-45 years	1.7	1.3
Older than 65 years	2.8	0.8*
All	2.2	1.5

Statistically not significant

Since the weight for waiting time for elderly is statistically not significant, two cases are studied:

1. Minimisation of total costs given a fixed demand level (O6.2) and assuming a fixed frequency. In this case only the weight for access time is relevant.

2. Minimisation of weighted door-to-door travel time given the budget determined in Chapter 7 (O2): both the access time and the waiting time are included in the optimisation.

The consequences of considering different user groups for the optimal stop and line spacing for a bus network are shown in Figure 9-5. The results for a tram network are similar. For adults and travellers having a car in-vehicle time and waiting time are more important, which results in coarser networks. Travellers without a car and elderly on the other hand, have a larger weight for walking, leading to denser networks. In general, the variation as a result of selecting specific populations is small compared to the impact of adopting the optimal values given one of these objectives instead of using traditional values for stop and line spacing. As expected, the network parameters for travellers older than 65 years are an exception, caused by the low weight for waiting time, which was statistically not significant. Intuitively, it might be questioned whether elderly really have uch a low weight for waiting time.

Of course, this analysis shows the extremes of opting for specific traveller groups in public transport network design. A more formal approach in which account is taken of different traveller groups simultaneously, using for instance Equation (9-5), will lead to smaller variations.

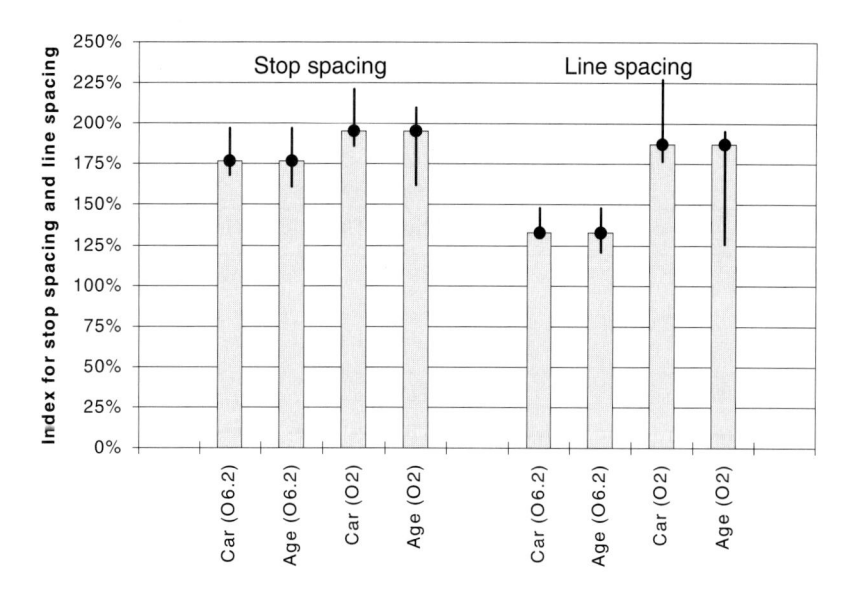

Chapter 9 Further analyses using analytical models 89

Figure 9-5: Influence of traveller groups on optimal stop and line spacing for bus networks

9.5 Impact of a multimodal approach

In all models discussed up until now, it is assumed that all travellers walk to the nearest stop. In practice, however, travellers may choose another mode to access the public transport system, especially in the case of trips starting at home. What would happen if, for instance, travellers would use a bicycle to arrive at the nearest stop? First, the extreme case that all travellers use bicycle is analysed. Second, an analysis is made for more realistic shares of cycling as an access mode. Third, an analysis is made of the impact on the demand for public transport. Finally, a more formal approach is presented.

9.5.1 Cycling instead of walking

For this extreme case it is assumed that all travellers use a bicycle to access the public transport line. The access speed will increase from 4 km/h up to 16 km/h, which allows for larger values for stop spacing and line spacing.

Table 9-7 and Figure 9-6 show the network characteristics for the traditional tram network and for optimal networks under different assumptions with regard to the access mode. The optimal values are determined using the two-step method described in Chapter 7:

1. Minimisation of total costs using a fixed demand pattern (O6.2);
2. Minimisation total travel time (O2) using the operational budget determined in step 1.

Table 9-7: Results for tram network for the access modes walking and cycling (trip length: 5 kilometres)

	Traditional	Min. Travel time	Min. Travel time
Access mode	Walking	Walking	Cycling
Demand		fixed	fixed
Stop spacing *(m)*	**400**	800	1500
Line spacing *(m)*	**1000**	900	2450
Stop density *(/km^2)*	**2.5**	1.4	0.3
Line density *(km/km^2)*	**1.0**	1.1	0.4
Frequency *(veh/h)*	**6.0**	6.0	9.0
Travel time *(min)*	26.3	23.9	19.6
Weighted travel time *(min)*	35.4	34.4	26.8
Operator costs *(fl/km^2)*	189	**153**	70
Cost effectiveness	83%	102%	223%
Profit *(fl/km^2)*	-33	3	86
Total costs *(fl/km^2)*	927	869	629
Patronage	**125**	**125**	**125**
Operational costs per traveller *(fl)*	1.51	1.22	0.56
Total costs per traveller *(fl)*	7.42	6.95	5.03

Note: Exogenous input values are shown in bold print. Adopted parameter values are given in Table 7-1.

Travel times are reduced as well as operational costs. Shorter travel times make the public transport system more attractive and will finally result in more travellers. All in all, although it is clearly an extreme case, it seems to be very attractive.

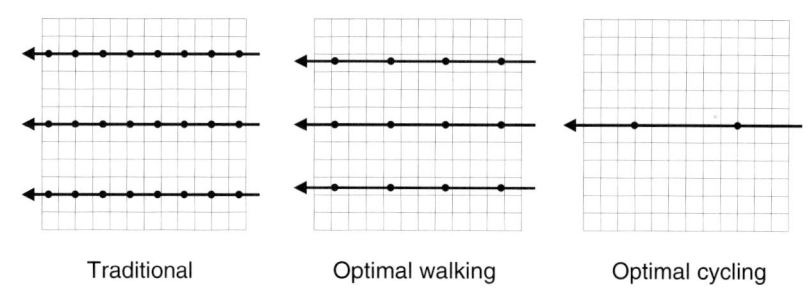

Chapter 9 Further analyses using analytical models 91

        Traditional   Optimal walking   Optimal cycling

Figure 9-6: Three network structures for a tram network with different access modes

There are, however, two important arguments in opposition to this line of reasoning. First, the maximum access distance is less than 2 kilometres. For such short distances, walking is still an important mode, even for unimodal trips (see also Schäffeler (1999)). The Dutch National Travel Survey, for instance, shows that walking accounts for 37 % of trips up to 2.5 kilometres and for 59 % of trips shorter than 1 kilometre. These percentages are based on all trips. For access trips it might be assumed that the percentage walking might even be higher, for instance, due to the fact that the bicycle must be parked at the bus stop. A clearly more realistic assumption would be that only part of the travellers would use other access modes than walking, dependent on the access distance.

Second, larger values for stop spacing and line spacing lead to larger access distances. Travellers who are forced to walk to the public transport system will have to walk longer distances, which will possibly result in longer travel times. As a result the coarser public transport system might be less attractive for them, which might lead to a loss of patronage too. Typical examples of travellers in this category are elderly, about 17 % of all public transport travellers, or travellers who have no bicycle available. Van der Waard (1988) found that only 62 % of travellers in urban public transport stated that they could have used a bicycle instead.

9.5.2 Realistic shares for cycling

What is then a realistic share for cycling as an access mode? Given the maximum access distance found for the case that all travellers cycle to the stop, and given the findings in the Dutch National Travel Survey, it can be assumed that even in this extreme case at least 37 % of the passengers will still walk. Thus, only 63 % of the travellers will use a bicycle to access the public transport system. Since all objectives are concerned with access time, the average access speed should be calculated as the harmonic mean for both access modes.

In the case that 37 % of the travellers will walk, the access speed will be about 8 km/h. The optimal value for stop spacing then becomes 1050 metres and for line spacing 1450 metres. The resulting maximum access distance is thus 1250 metres. For this access distance, however, it is a more realistic assumption that only 41 % of the travellers use other access modes than walking, leading to an average access speed of 6 km/h.

Table 9-8: Results for both network types for mixed access modes walking and cycling (O6.2 and O2)

	Bus (trip length 3 km.)			Tram (trip length 5 km.)		
	Traditional	Min. Travel time	Min. Travel time	Traditional	Min. Travel time	Min. Travel time
Average access speed *(km/h)*	4	4	6	4	4	6
Demand		fixed	fixed	fixed	fixed	fixed
Stop spacing *(m)*	**350**	700	850	**400**	800	950
Line spacing *(m)*	**500**	900	1250	**1000**	900	1200
Stop density *(/km²)*	5.7	1.6	0.9	2.5	1.4	0.9
Line density *(km/km²)*	2.0	1.1	0.8	1.0	1.1	0.8
Frequency *(veh/h)*	4.0	5.9	6.6	6.0	6.0	7.0
Travel time *(min)*	22.1	20.1	18.4	26.3	23.9	21.6
Weighted travel time *(min)*	30.0	30.2	27.3	35.4	34.4	30.5
Operator costs *(fl/km²)*	163	95	71	189	153	126
Cost effectiveness	46%	79%	106%	83%	102%	124%
Profit *(fl/km²)*	-88	-20	4	-33	3	30
Total costs *(fl/km²)*	663	598	526	927	870	761
Patronage	**100**	**100**	**100**	**125**	**125**	**125**
Operational costs per traveller *(fl)*	1.63	0.95	0.71	1.51	1.22	1.01
Total costs per traveller *(fl)*	6.63	5.98	5.26	7.41	6.96	6.09

Note: Exogenous input values are shown in bold print. Adopted parameter values are given in Table 7-1.

Table 9-8 and Figure 9-7 show the network characteristics given this average access speed for both the bus and the tram network, again using the two-step procedure described before. Compared to the extreme case presented in Table 9-7, the impact on stop and line spacing is clearly less, but the reductions of travel times and operational costs are still significant. Given these reductions of travel times, the assumption of a fixed demand is of course not realistic. In the next section the impact of other access modes on the demand level is analysed further.

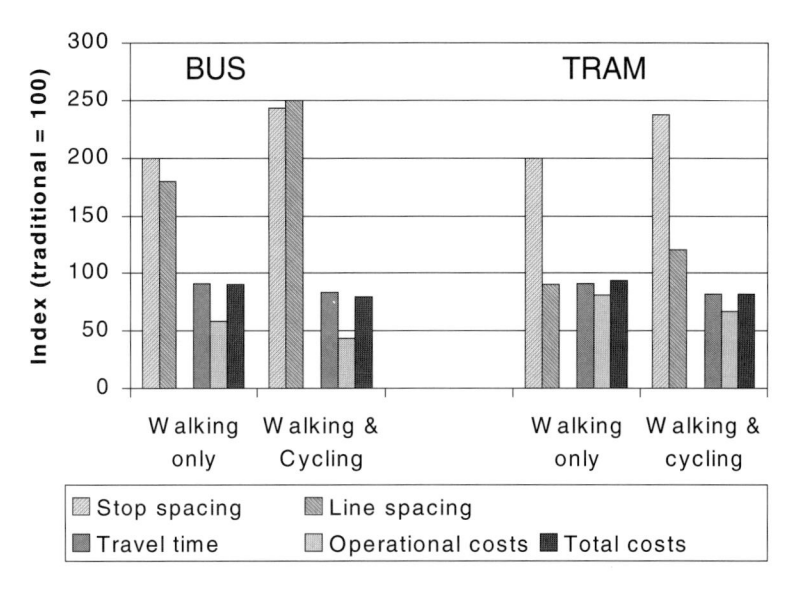

Chapter 9 Further analyses using analytical models   93

Figure 9-7: Main characteristics of optimised networks with and without cycling as an access mode (O6.2 and O2)

9.5.3 Impact on demand level

Basically, there are two groups of travellers that can be distinguished:

- Travellers who can choose which mode they will use to access the public transport system depending on access distance. They will experience shorter travel times, which will increase demand;
- Travellers who are forced to walk to the nearest stop regardless of access distance. These travellers will have longer travel times, which will decrease demand.

For both groups the weighted travel times are calculated for the networks found in the previous section, using Equation (4-6) and their respective access speed, that is 6 and 4 kilometres per hour respectively. Using these weighted travel times and the logit mode-choice model described with Equation (4-7), the consequences for the demand level can be determined. Since the net effect depends on the share of travellers who are not able to use other access modes, four different scenarios are presented in Figure 9-8. It is clear that even using cautious assumptions with regard to the average access speed and to the share of travellers who can choose their access mode, the demand for public transport increases. For small cities the net effect might be limited but for large cities, the increase is interesting. This is certainly true if the reductions in operational costs of 20 % up to 25 % are considered too.

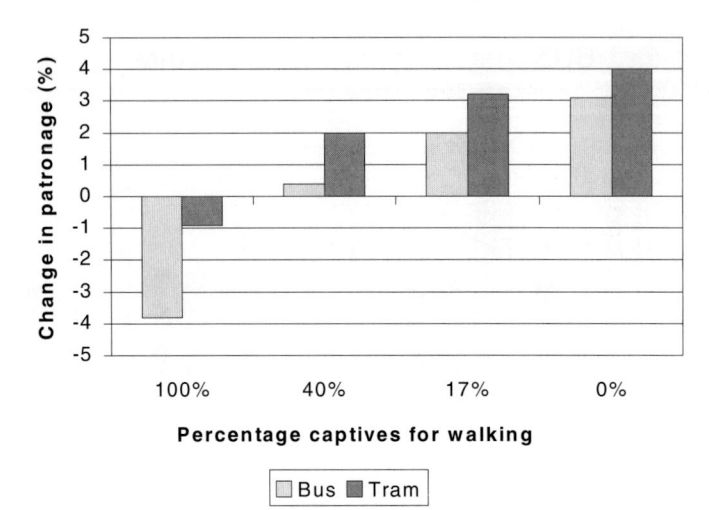

Figure 9-8: Net impact on demand level of a multimodal network structure for four access scenarios

9.5.4 Formal approach

The analyses in the previous sections are more conceptual. The advantage of this approach is that is clearly shows two important aspects when considering multimodal concepts for urban public transport. First, walking will always be an important access mode, which reduces the impact on the optimal network characteristics, and second, the possible increase in patronage due to the shorter door-to-door travel times will be limited.

The concept of using different modes to access the public transport system can also be analysed more formally. The main difference is that a distinction must be made between the populations using each mode, that is P_1 and P_2. Each of these populations has its own access time determined by the access distance D_a and the access speed v_{aj}. The weighted door-to-door travel time can then be written as:

$$T_c = w_a \cdot \frac{D_a}{v_{a1}} \cdot \frac{P_1}{P} + w_a \cdot \frac{D_a}{v_{a2}} \cdot \frac{P_2}{P} + w_w \cdot T_w + \frac{D_c}{D_s} \cdot \left(\frac{D_s}{v} + T_s \right) + w_e \cdot T_e \qquad (9\text{-}9)$$

where:
$$D_a = f_a \cdot (D_s + D_l)$$
$$P = P_1 + P_2$$

The size of these sub-populations will depend on the access time per mode, which can be described using the logit-mode-choice model (see also Equation (4-7)):

Chapter 9 Further analyses using analytical models

$$P_1 = \frac{\exp\left(-\alpha_1 \cdot \dfrac{D_a}{v_{a1}}\right)}{\exp\left(-\alpha_1 \cdot \dfrac{D_a}{v_{a1}}\right) + \exp\left(-\alpha_2 \cdot \dfrac{D_a}{v_{a2}} - \varphi\right)} \cdot P \qquad (9\text{-}10)$$

The constant φ is introduced to prevent that the share of walking drops too fast. An example of this function using values that lead to a good agreement with the modal split found in the Dutch National Travel Survey is given in Figure 9-9.

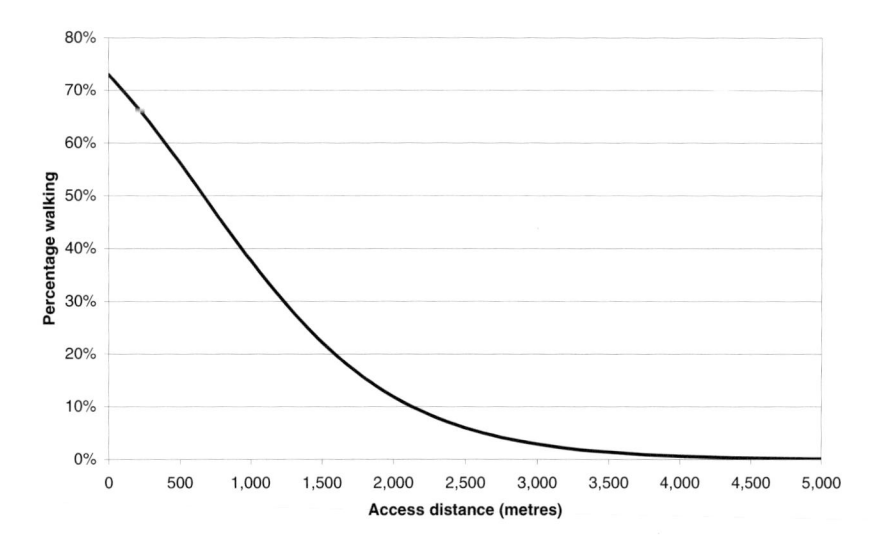

Figure 9-9: Percentage of public transport users who walk to the stop as a function of the access distance ($\alpha_1=0.12$, $\alpha_2=0.08$, $\varphi=1$)

Equation (9-9) can be simplified by introducing the average access speed $\bar{v}_a$, which is calculated using the weighted harmonic mean of the access speeds:

$$\bar{v}_a = \frac{P}{\dfrac{P_1}{v_{a1}} + \dfrac{P_2}{v_{a2}}} \qquad (9\text{-}11)$$

This results in the following equation for the weighted door-to-door travel time:

$$T_c = w_a \cdot \frac{D_a}{\bar{v}_a} + w_w \cdot T_w + \frac{D_c}{D_s} \cdot \left(\frac{D_s}{v} + T_s\right) + w_e \cdot T_e \qquad (9\text{-}12)$$

The latter equation was used in the previous sections given the assumption of a fixed demand. The analysis of the impact on the demand level showed that the changes in the demand level are small, and that, therefore, the assumption of a fixed demand level is certainly justified.

Using these equations, however, it is also possible to analyse what the outcome would be if the demand depends on the quality of the services offered. Equation (9-10) is used to determine which share of the total population walks to the stop and which share uses the bicycle. Given these shares Equation (9-11) is used to calculate the resulting average access speed, which is then used in Equation (9-12). Given this formulation of the weighted door-to-door travel time objective functions such as maximising profit, maximising cost effectiveness, and maximising social welfare, can be optimised using enumeration.

The shapes of the objective functions are more or less identical to those shown in Chapter 6. The objective functions for maximising profit, maximising social welfare, and minimising total costs are all flat around the optimum. The main difference compared to the original situation of walking only is that an increase in access distance, has less influence on the demand. As a result the shape of the objective function maximising demand is more flat, as is shown in Figure 9-10.

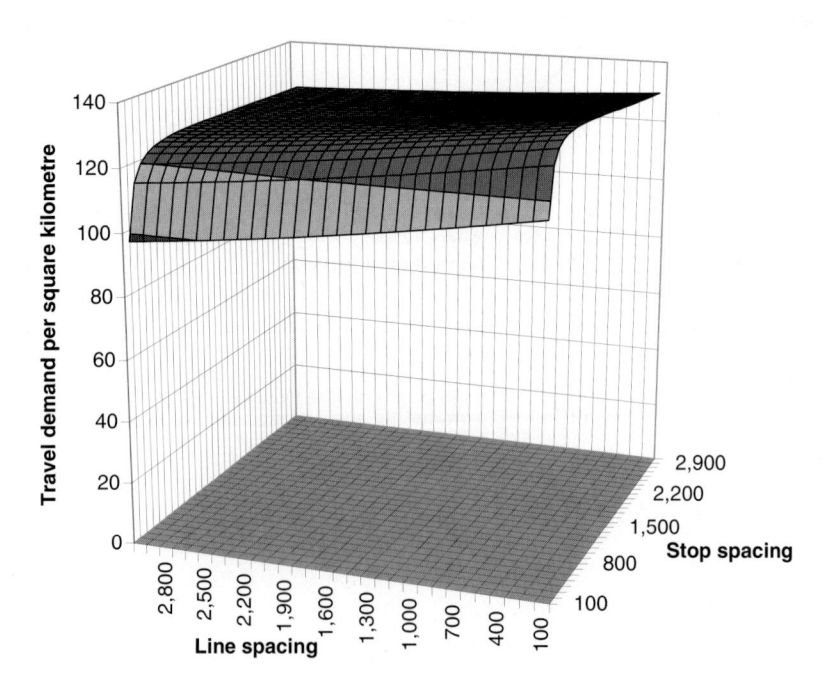

Figure 9-10: O7: Maximising travel demand (logit) in the case of two access modes

For this analysis the preferred objective of maximising social welfare is used. Since frequencies are relevant in a multimodal context, an additional analysis is made for which frequency social welfare is maximal. In this analysis the values of 4, 6, 8, and 10 vehicles

Chapter 9 Further analyses using analytical models

are used. As could be expected from the results of Section 7.2, a frequency of 6 vehicles per hour is optimal for a bus network having the access mode walking only. The same result was found for a tram network. In the case of cycling as an additional access mode, the optimal frequency is 8 vehicles per hour for both cases.

Table 9-9: Results for both network types for mixed access modes walking and cycling (O5)

	Bus (trip length 3 km.)			Tram (trip length 5 km.)		
	Traditional	Max. Social welfare	Max. Social welfare	Traditional	Max. Social welfare	Max. Social welfare
Average access speed *(km/h)*	4.0	4.0	6.0	4.0	4.0	6.3
Percentage walking	100%	100%	55%	100%	100%	52%
Stop spacing *(m)*	350	600	900	400	800	1,100
Line spacing *(m)*	500	800	1,200	1,000	900	1,400
Stop density *(/km^2)*	5.7	2.1	0.9	2.5	1.4	0.6
Line density *(km/km^2)*	2.0	1.3	0.8	1.0	1.1	0.7
Frequency *(veh/h)*	4	6	8	6	6	8
Travel time *(min)*	22.1	19.7	17.5	26.3	23.9	21.3
Weighted travel time *(min)*	30.0	28.8	26.0	35.4	34.4	30.6
Operator costs *(fl/km^2)*	163	116	88	189	153	118
Cost effectiveness	46%	66%	89%	83%	103%	137%
Profit *(fl/km^2)*	-88	-40	-10	-33	4	44
Total costs *(fl/km^2)*	663	604	546	927	875	781
Patronage	100	102	105	125	126	130
Operational costs per traveller *(fl)*	1.63	1.14	0.84	1.51	1.21	0.91
Total costs per traveller *(fl)*	6.63	5.92	5.20	7.42	6.94	6.01

Note: Exogenous input values are shown in bold print. Adopted parameter values are given in Table 7-1.

The results for this analysis are shown in Table 9-9 and Figure 9-11. Compared to traditional design stop spacing is nearly tripled, while line spacing is more than doubled for bus networks and increases with 40 % for tram networks. Travel times are reduced with more than 10 %, and the operational costs drop to slightly more than 50 % for bus networks and to about 65 % for tram networks.

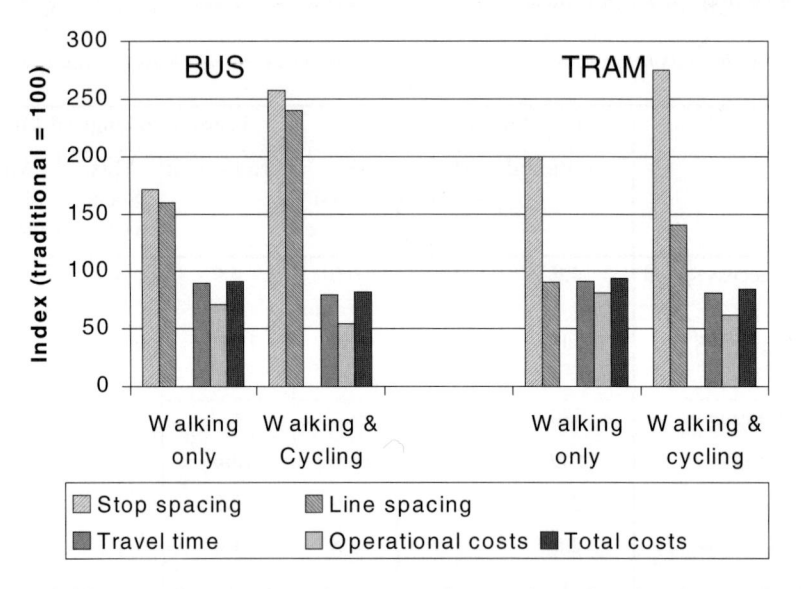

Figure 9-11: Main characteristics for optimised networks with and without cycling as an access mode (O5)

The consequences of this more detailed approach are different for the bus and the tram network. In the case of the bus network, the network structure is nearly identical to the structure found in Section 9.5.2. The only difference is the higher frequency, which results in higher operational costs too. The sum of traveller's costs and operator's costs, however, is slightly reduced. The optimal network structure for the tram network, on the other hand, is coarser than in the case of a fixed demand. Due to the larger stop and line spacing the operational costs are reduced, even though the frequency is increased. In this case however, the total costs are slightly increased.

9.5.5 Conclusions

The results of the pragmatic and the formal approach are consistent. Walking will always be an important access mode. If it is assumed that all travellers do choose between walking and cycling, the share of walking will be 50 % up to 60 %. A multimodal approach then results in coarser networks that are more attractive for travellers and have lower operational costs. The expected increase in patronage is limited to 5 %. It is unknown, however, whether travellers really consider cycling as an alternative mode to access urban public transport. More research on traveller behaviour is necessary to determine whether there is a population that is captive with respect to walking, and what the size of that population is.

Chapter 9 Further analyses using analytical models   99

Given the positive results with respect to the weighted door-to-door travel time, stimulating and encouraging of cycling as an access mode is certainly worthwhile. A possible strategy might be to use the results of the analysis of cycling only to determine which stops should be equipped with facilities for parking bicycles. In that case stop spacing is doubled and line spacing is nearly tripled, which results in parking facilities for one out of six stops. Given the fact that cycling to the destination is also an alternative for public transport usage, it is clear that this approach should be applied for stops at a certain distance from the city centre. Cycling as an access mode might therefore be more interesting for a tram network than for a bus network.

Chapter 10

CONCLUSIONS AND FURTHER RESEARCH

This report discussed the design problem for urban public transport networks for different design objectives. Optimisation models have been established for determining optimal values for the key design parameters for pubic transport network design, that is, stop spacing and line spacing, and implicitly frequency too, given certain objective functions. Examples of objective functions are minimising weighted door-to-door travel time, maximising profit, and maximising social welfare.

In order to study the characteristics of these optimisation models a number of applications for a bus and a tram network were performed. Furthermore, the models were extended to a complete network, and to daily operations, an analysis is made of the influence of distinguishing different traveller groups, and a detailed analysis is made of the impact of multimodal access to stops.

This chapter summarises the main conclusions, with a distinction between a theoretical and a practical point of view, and presents recommendations for further research.

10.1 Theoretical conclusions

The choice of an objective as a basis for public transport network design proves to be essential. The objectives that have been shown to be most suitable for urban public transport network design are maximising social welfare, which is the sum of consumer surplus and operator surplus, and minimising total costs, that is, the sum of traveller costs and operator costs, given a fixed level of demand. They result in the overall best combination of attractiveness and performance. For analytical purposes, minimising total costs, which is more tractable and requires less data, is a good second-best approach.

The main characteristic of these preferred objectives is that a balance is found between the interests of the traveller and the operator. Objectives that focus on one of these parties only always lead to network designs that are optimal for one party and are unattractive for the other.

Traditional network design characteristics can be replicated by focussing on short trips only, and by opting for the objective of minimising weighted door-to-door travel time only, and thereby ignoring operational costs. Focussing on longer trips only results already in an increase of the stop spacing of 40 % up to 50 % (see also Figure 10-1). Inclusion of the operational costs in the design objective, such as for instance in the objective of maximising social welfare leads to an additional increase of 30 % up to 50 % for the stop spacing. The assumption of alternative access modes yields a further increase of 80 %.

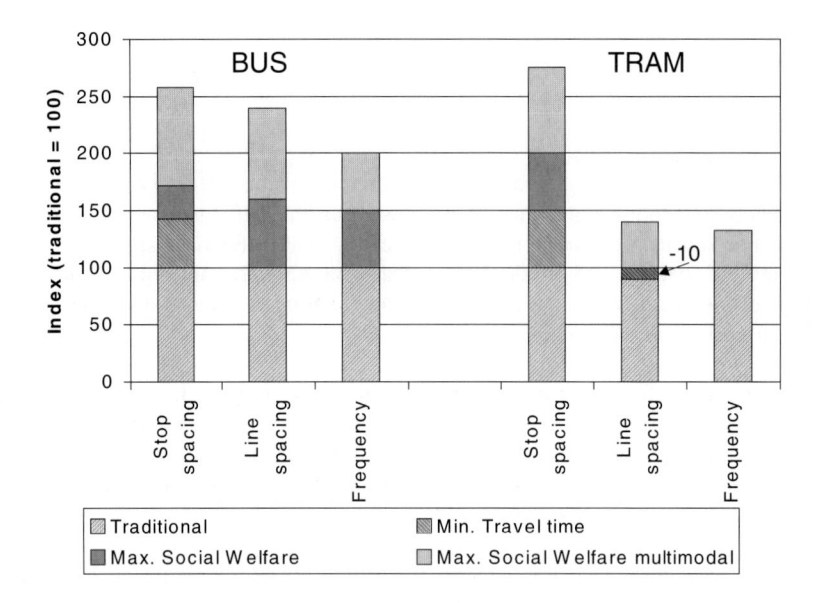

Figure 10-1: Impact of various assumptions on the optimal values for stop spacing, line spacing, and frequency (please note that in the case of maximising social welfare for the tram network, the line spacing is reduced with 10 %)

In the case of the bus network, the frequency proved to be an important decision variable too. Maximising social welfare, thus including operational costs too, resulted in an increase of the line spacing of 60 % leading to a frequency of 6 vehicles per hour.

It is interesting to notice that the optimal values for stop and line spacing of the bus network are almost identical to those for the tram network. Apparently, a tram network is equivalent to a bus network having only higher demand and higher trip lengths, which compensate the higher operational costs. The average costs per traveller for a tram network are slightly higher than those for the bus network. However, if the trip length is taken into account, the bus networks proves to be more expensive per kilometre travelled.

The models presented in this report can also be used in the case that frequencies are a design variable too. For instance, the frequencies can be determined simultaneously with the values for stop spacing and line spacing using the objective of minimising total costs, given a fixed level of demand.

If the objective of minimising total costs is used, modelling the level of demand in an analytical optimisation model for urban public transport networks has a limited influence on the results. It is even possible that the increase in travel time is more than compensated by the reduction in patronage, because of which no optimum can be found. Modelling travel demand for this objective is therefore relevant from a theoretical point of view only.

Extension of the model to a network, in which radial and transversal trips are considered simultaneously, leads to slightly coarser public transport networks. Trip lengths and the importance of waiting time increases, while the importance of access time is reduced, which overall yields larger values for stop and line spacing.

The impact of designing an urban public transport network for specific groups of travellers is less than the choice for a specific objective, that is compared to traditional design. Given a specific objective the maximum deviation of the stop spacing as a result of opting for specific traveller groups is 15 %. For line spacing the maximum deviation is 30 %. It should be noted, however, that the relationships found for the optimal network parameters show that using lower values for the network design parameters leads to a larger impact on the value of the objective function than using higher values. Opting for elderly, for instance, results in lower values for stop and line spacing, which might be less optimal due to the large discrepancy with other traveller groups, than opting for the 'average' traveller. In the latter case the discrepancies in optimal values are smaller, and for the part of the travellers that prefer lower values the impact on their objective is small.

A multimodal approach for the access to urban public transport leads, as expected, to larger stop spacing and line spacing, but the increase is limited, that is compared to the situation that all travellers would cycle to the stops. A large share of travellers, at least 50 %, will still walk to the stop, which reduces the average access speed significantly. The resulting network characteristics, however, are still 30 % to 40 % larger than those for the optimal network in the case of walking only, leading to shorter travel times and lower operational costs.

10.2 Recommendations for planning practice

Currently applied values for stop and line spacing are too small and should be increased to achieve lower operational costs and more attractive public transport networks (see also Figure 10-2). For a bus network the stop spacing should be preferably 600 up to 700 metres, and for tram networks stop spacing should be 800 metres. The line spacing for bus networks should be doubled to 1.000 metres in order to increase the frequencies to 6 vehicles per hour. Apparently, current urban public transport network designs focus to much on accessibility of stops or on short trip lengths, while operational costs seem to play a marginal role.

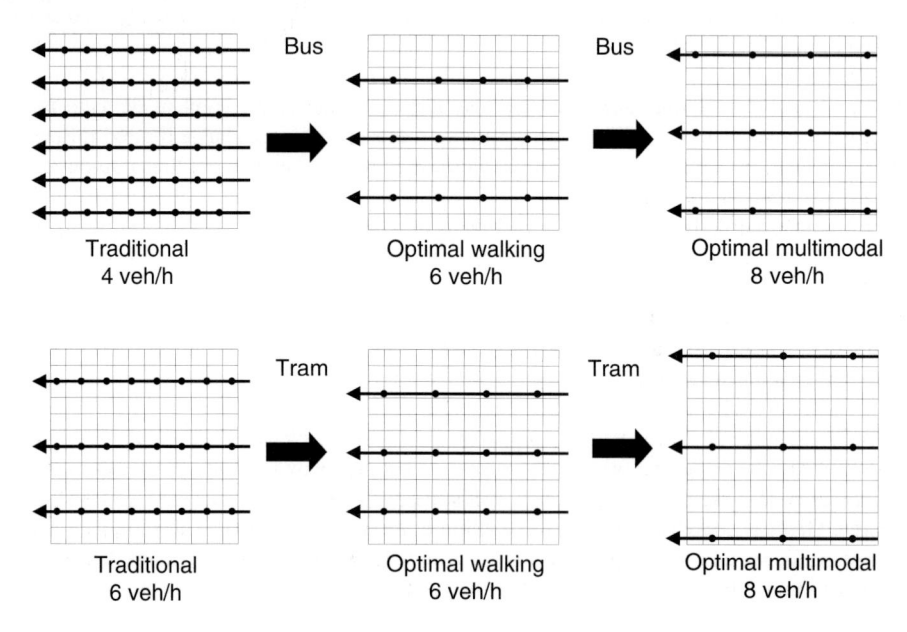

Figure 10-2: Spatial characteristics of optimised networks compared to traditional design

These optimal values for stop spacing and line spacing should not be used as rigid values but as averages that may be adjusted locally to account for local characteristics. It has been shown that the values for the stop spacing can be applied in a realistic case for the city of The Hague in the Netherlands, and it is expected that, generally, there will be no practical constraints for adopting these design principles as a guideline in planning processes. For the line spacing, however, it might be difficult in some cases to adopt the optimal values, for instance, because of the characteristics of the existing road network. In these cases the proposed increase in stop spacing might be limited to 450 metres for bus networks and 600 metres for tram networks.

The sensitivity analysis, the analysis of the extension to a network and to daily operations, and the impact of multimodal access to the stops, show that the assumptions used in the analysis can be considered to be rather conservative. More progressive assumptions, for instance, with respect to the allocation of stops or the access speed, leads to even coarser networks. This is certainly true for the stop spacing, since the assumptions that are most likely to be a subject for discussion, that is, the number of travellers that is assumed and the level of the operational costs, mostly influence the value of the optimal line spacing.

Chapter 10 Conclusions and further research 105

The stop spacing in city centres should at least remain constant and should certainly not decrease compared to the stop spacing outside the city centre. Shorter stop spacing in city centres might be advantageous for travellers who have their destination in the borders of the city centre, but is bad for long-distance travellers who travel through the city centre.

In the case that, due to company policy or local politicians, other design objectives are chosen, or that the network is designed for specific groups of travellers, the models presented in this report can be used to estimate the impact of these decisions on the network performance characteristics. Comparison of the network characteristics given the applied design variables with those given the optimal values presented in this report, shows the consequences for the cost effectiveness and the necessary level of subsidy.

Profit maximisation has been shown to lead to profitable networks that are, however, not attractive for the traveller. The introduction of a subsidy per traveller has more influence on the level of profit than on the network structure. These findings imply that a commercial approach of urban public transport will lead to socially sub-optimal network structures. Authorities have therefore an important role in guaranteeing an urban public transport network that is optimal from a social point of view.

Stimulating and encouraging the use of other modes to access the public transport system would make the public transport system more attractive while offering further possibilities to reduce operational costs significantly. Since the optimal urban public transport network having cycling as the only access mode yields a doubling of the stop spacing and nearly a tripling of the line spacing, it might be an interesting strategy to provide one out of six stops with facilities for parking bicycles.

10.3 Recommendations for further research

An important assumption in this study is the way the weighted travel time is formulated and the value of the coefficients that are used. In this study values are used, which are determined for urban public transport in the Netherlands, using a similar formulation of the weighted travel time. These assumptions are therefore as realistic as possible. However, there are three aspects that deserve more attention:

1. The study of Van der Waard (1988) in which he weights for the various time elements were determined, considers mostly access distances between 100 and 500 metres, although larger values ranging up to 900 metres are included too. It might be questioned whether the weights found by Van der Waard still hold in the case of large access distances.

2. The model implicitly assumes that there is a linear relationship for all time elements. An alternative assumption might be that there is a non-linear relationship in which short access distances have a lower weight than long access distances.

3. There is insufficient knowledge of traveller behaviour with respect to using other modes to access urban public transport.

The SMM-project "SMM-1: Travel demand modelling" will analyse these aspects further, using new techniques to describe travel behaviour (fuzzy logic, see for instance Hoogendoorn-Lanser & Hoogendoorn (2000)) and using new empirical data.

The issue of different levels in public transport systems in large urban areas or agglomerations is still unclear. Egeter (1993) found that a second network level would be realistic for cities having a radius larger than 8 kilometres. Egeter did not, however, analyse the consequences of this second level for the performance of the first network level. Alternative approaches for urban agglomerations are the introduction of feeder lines or the introduction of the concept of zonal transit. There is already literature with regard to analytical models on both issues. However, a comparison between these approaches has not been made yet.

The presented models may also be extended to a formal description of a hierarchical multi-layer network. In that case there is a set of networks, each having their own functional characteristics, and there is a hierarchical relationship between these networks. Network i is not only an option for a specific type of trips, but network i is also an access network for higher order network $i+1$. If, for simplicity sake, the simple objective of minimising travel time only is used (O1), the design problem for network i can be formulated as minimising the following objective function (see also Equation (5-1)):

$$T_{t,i} = w_{a,i} \cdot \frac{f_{a,i} \cdot 2 \cdot D_{s,i}}{v_{a,i}} + \frac{D_{c,i}}{D_{s,i}} \cdot \left(\frac{D_{s,i}}{v_i} + T_{s,i} \right) + T_{we,i} \tag{10-1}$$

in which $v_{a,i}$ can be described by:

$$v_{a,i} = \frac{w_{a,i-1} \cdot \frac{f_{a,i-1} \cdot 2 \cdot D_{s,i-1}}{v_{a,i-1}} + \frac{D_{c,i-1}}{D_{s,i-1}} \cdot \left(\frac{D_{s,i-1}}{v_{i-1}} + T_{s,i-1} \right) + T_{we,i-1}}{D_{c,i-1}} \tag{10-2}$$

Such a model implies a recursive relationship between the different networks, that is, the characteristics of the lower order network determine the characteristics of the higher order network. Furthermore, there exists a strong dependency between the different spatial levels that are assumed. This is especially true for the average travel distances, but also for parameters such as the access factor f_a.

Both aspects, the comparison of various network concepts as well as the hierarchical multi-layer network structure, will be analysed further in the SMM-project 'Design of Multimodal Transport Systems'.

References

BLACK A. (1978)
Optimizing urban mass transit systems: a general model
Transportation Research Record **677**, pp. 41-47

BRÄNDLI H., M. GLASER, G. JUNKER (1980)
Optimale Haltenstellenabstände beim öffentlichen Verkehr
Forschungsauftrag 25/70, Schlussbericht
Vereinigung Schweizerischer Verkehrsingenieure, Zurich

CARAMIA M., P. CAROTENUTO, G. CONFESSORE (1998)
An iterative scheme for bus network optimisation problems
Paper presented at the 6th Meeting of the EURO Working group on Transportation, Göteborg

CARRESE S., S. GORI (1998)
An urban bus network design procedure
Paper presented at the 6th Meeting of the EURO Working group on Transportation, Göteborg

CEDER A., Y. ISRAELI (1998)
User and operator perspectives in transit network design
Transportation Research Record **1623** pp.3-7

CHANG S.K., P.M. SCHONFELD (1991)
Optimization models for comparing conventional and subscription bus feeder services
Transportation Science, Vol. **25**, *No. 4, pp. 281-298*

CHANG S.K., P.M. SCHONFELD (1993A)
Optimal dimensions of bus service zones
Journal of Transportation Engineering Vol. **119**, *No. 4, pp. 567-585*

CHANG S.K., P.M. SCHONFELD (1993B)
Welfare maximization with financial constraints for bus transit systems
Transportation Research Record **1395**, pp. 48-57

CHANG S.K., W.J. YU (1996)
Comparison of subsidized fixed- and flexible-route bus systems
Transportation Research Record **1557**, pp. 15-20

DAGANZO C.F. (1999)
Logistic systems analysis, third edition
Springer, Berlin

DE HEIJ H.T.A., J.H.M. MAASSEN (1995)
Almere: Hoogwaardig openbaar vervoer in de praktijk
Verkeerskunde Vol. **46**, *No. 7/8, pp.44-48*

EGETER B. (1993)
Systeemopbouw in stedelijke gebieden
Report VK 5115.301, TU Delft, Delft

EGETER B. (1995)
Optimizing public transport structure in urban areas
Proceedings of Transportation Congress, Volume 2, San Diego

FURTH P.G., A.B. RAHBEE (2000)
Optimal bus stop spacing using dynamic programming and geographic modeling
Paper 00-0870, CD-ROM of the 79th annual meeting of the Transportation Research Board, Washington

GHONEIM N.S., S.C. WIRASINGHE (1987)
Optimum zone configuration for planned urban commuter rail lines
Transportation Science, Vol. 21, No. 2, pp. 106-114

HOLROYD E.M. (1967)
The optimum bus service: a theoretical model for a large uniform urban area
Vehicular traffic science, Proceedings of the 3rd Int. Symposium on the Theory of Traffic Flow
Elsevier, New York

HOOGENDOORN-LANSER S., S.P. HOOGENDOORN
Genetic fuzzy travel choice behaviour modeling for public transport networks
Paper 00-0914, CD-ROM of the 79th annual meeting of the Transportation Research Board, Washington

KOCUR G., C. HENDRICKSON (1982)
Design of local bus service with demand equilibration
Transportation Science, Vol. 16, No. 2, pp. 149-170

KOOT A., B. GOVERS (1995)
Systeemopbouw openbaar vervoer in de praktijk
Verkeerskunde Vol. 46, No. 7/8, pp. 26-30

KUAH G.K., J. PERL (1988)
Optimization of feeder bus routes and bus-stop spacing
Journal of Transportation Engineering, Vol. 114, No. 3, pp. 341-354

LIU G., G. QUAIN, S.C. WIRASINGHE (1996)
Rail line length in a crosstown corridor with many-to-many demand
Journal of Advanced Transportation, Vol. 30, No. 1, pp. 95-114

NEWELL G.F. (1979)
Some issues relating to the optimal design of bus routes
Transportation Science, Vol. 13, No. 1, pp. 20-35

PROJECTBUREAU IVVS (1995)
Aspecten bij het ontwerpen van netwerken voor het stads- en streekvervoer
Ministry of transport, public works and watermanagement, Den Haag

PROJECTBUREAU TRAM PLUS (1994)
Tram Plus, De metamorfose van de tram
Projectbureau Tram Plus, Rotterdam

ROEDOE A. (1995)
Grofweg beter, een case-studie naar een nieuw stedelijk OV-netwerk
Report VK 5115.701, TU Delft, Delft

SCHÄFFELER U. (1999)
Optimale Haltestellenabstände für den öffentlichen Nahverkehr in den Niederlanden unter spezieller Beachtung des multimodalen Verkehrs, Master's thesis
ETH Zürich/TU Delft, Faculty of Civil Engineering, Delft

SPASOVIC L.N., M.P. BOILE, A.K. BLADIKAS (1994)
Bus transit service coverage for maximum profit and social welfare
Transportation Research Record **1451**, *pp. 12-22*

SPASOVIC L.N., P.M. SCHONFELD (1993)
Method for optimizing transit service coverage
Transportation Research Record **1402**, *pp. 28-39*

STADSGEWEST HAAGLANDEN (1999)
AggloNet bereikt meer
Stadsgewest Haaglanden, Den Haag

TSAO S., P. SCHONFELD (1983)
Optimization of zonal transit service
Journal of Transportation Engineering, Vol. **109**, *No. 2, pp. 257-272*

TSAO S., P. SCHONFELD (1984)
Branched transit services: an analysis
Journal of Transportation Engineering, Vol. **110**, *No. 1, pp. 112-128*

VAN DER WAARD J. (1988)
Onderzoek weging tijdelementen, Deelrapport 3: Analyse routekeuzegedrag van openbaar vervoerreizigers
Report VK 5302.303, TU Delft, Delft

VAN GOEVERDEN C.D., M.G. VAN DEN HEUVEL (1993)
De verplaatsingstijdfactor in verhouding tot de vervoerwijzekeuze
Report VK 5304.301, TU Delft, Delft

VAN NES R., R. HAMERSLAG, L.H. IMMERS (1988)
Design of public transport networks
Transportation Research Record **1202**, *pp. 74-83*

VAN NES R. (1998)
Analytical optimisation models for the design of transportation networks
Proceedings of the 4-th TRAIL PhD-Congress 1998, Part 2
TRAIL, Delft

VAN NES R. (1999)
Design of multimodal transport systems, Setting the scene, Review of literature and basic concepts
TRAIL Studies in Transportation Science S99/3, TRAIL, Delft

WALTHER K. (1973)
Nachfrageorientierte Bewertung der Streckenführung im öffentlichen Personennahverkehr
Veröffentlichen des Verkehrswissenschaftlichen Institutes der RWTH Aachen, Aachen

WIRASINGHE S.C. (1980)
Nearly optimal parameters for a rail/feeder-bus system on a rectangular grid
Transportation Research Part A, Vol. 14, No. 1, pp. 33-40

WIRASINGHE S.C., N.S. GHONEIM (1981)
Spacing of bus-stops for many to many travel demand
Transportation Science, Vol. 15, No. 3, pp. 210-221

WIRASINGHE S.C., P.N. SENEVIRATNE (1986)
Rail line length in an urban transportation corridor
Transportation Science, Vol. 20, No. 4, pp. 237-245

Appendix A
Argumentation for using average travel distances

In formulating the optimisation problem, we looked at a part of an urban area at an average distance D_c from the city centre. The use of an average travel distance suggests, that is doesn't matter how the demand is distributed along the line. It is clear that stops are only needed if there is sufficient demand for public transport, and that if there is no demand, or nearly no demand, no stops are necessary. In the case that the demand along the line is sufficient, it is the question whether the distribution of demand influences the optimal stop spacing.

In order to consider the distribution along the line, the line can be divided into an infinite number of segments for which the optimal stop spacing is determined. Each segment is weighted by the demand level for that segment. The objective function for minimisation of travel time (O1, see also Equation (6-4)) should then be written as:

$$T_t = \int_{x=0}^{D_{max}} \left(\kappa \cdot p(x) \cdot D_s + \frac{\lambda' \cdot x \cdot p(x)}{D_s} + \mu \right) d(x) \tag{A-1}$$

where:

$$\kappa = \frac{w_a \cdot f_a}{v_a}$$

$$\lambda' = T_s$$

$$\mu = \frac{w_w \cdot f_w}{F} + \frac{x}{v} + w_e \cdot T_e$$

$p(x)$ = demand for transit to the city centre at distance x

Equation (A-1) can be rewritten as:

$$T_t = \kappa \cdot D_s \cdot \int_{x=0}^{D_{max}} p(x)d(x) + \frac{\lambda'}{D_s} \cdot \int_{x=0}^{D_{max}} x \cdot p(x)d(x) + \int_{x=0}^{D_{max}} \mu d(x) \tag{A-2}$$

It can be seen that Equation (A-2) has the same format as Equation (6-4). Minimising Equation (A-2) with regard to D_s leads to the following relationship between the optimal stop spacing and the average travel distance:

$$D_s^{*2} = \frac{\beta'}{\alpha} \cdot \frac{\int_{x=0}^{D_{max}} x \cdot p(x)d(x)}{\int_{x=0}^{D_{max}} p(x)d(x)} = \frac{\beta'}{\alpha} \cdot \overline{D}_c \qquad (A-3)$$

where:

$\overline{D}_c$ = weigthed average travel distance to city centre

This result implies that the distance to the city centre D_c can be replaced by the weighted average travel distance of all trips to the city centre. Given the weighted average travel distance, the optimal stop spacing proves thus to be independent of the actual distribution of the demand pattern along the line. This conclusion, of course, does not hold if the stop spacing is assumed to be variable.

Appendix B
Derivation of the costs factors for bus and tram

The cost factors for bus and tram used in Chapter 7 are based on a macro model for calculating the operational costs and revenues for the HTM, that is the public transport company of The Hague. Input in this model is based on three sources:

- Annual report HTM (HTM (1999): Jaarverslag 1998, *NV Gemengd bedrijf Haagsche Tramweg Maatschappij*, Den Haag);
- Report on operational costs in urban public transport (Erkens A., P.B.L. Wiggenraad (1994): Onderzoek exploitatiekosten tram, metro, sneltram en bus, *Report VK 5901.301, TU Delft*, Delft);
- Rule of thumb.

The annual report (HTM (1999)) provides the following data

Passenger kilometres per year	393,000,000
Passenger revenues *(fl)*	94,293,133
Subsidy *(fl)*	201,990,820
Cost efficiency (passenger revenues/operational costs)	32 %
Number of busses	211
Number of trams	147
Driving staff	1.039
Total staff line bound public transport	1.979

The ratio of revenues and passenger kilometres yields the income per passenger kilometre:

- Revenue per passenger kilometre: *fl* 0.24;
- Subsidy per passenger kilometre: *fl* 0.51;
- Total income per passenger kilometre: *fl* 0,75.

The report on operational costs (Erkens & Wiggenraad (1994)) leads to the following cost factors per vehicle per hour:

- Bus: *fl* 135.00;
- Tram: *fl* 225.00.

A commonly used rule of thumb says that 2/3 of the operational costs is personnel. If this is combined with the ratio of line-bound personnel and driving staff, the total costs per vehicle per hour increase with 60 % to:

- Bus: *fl* 217.00;
- Tram: *fl* 362.00.

The basic unit in the macro model is the vehicle. Per vehicle type an estimate is made of patronage, revenues and operational costs for a typical peak hour, a normal hour and an off-peak hour. These results are aggregated to total incomes and costs per vehicle type for an average day. Multiplication with the number of vehicles per type results in the total incomes and costs per vehicle type. Addition of these subtotals yields the final result for the operator. This calculation is summarised in the following table:

	Peak hour	Normal hour	Off-peak hour	Working day	All vehicles
Number of hours per day	4	8	6	16	
Tram					
• Passengers per leg	**120**	**60**	**30**		
• Number of legs per hour	**3**	**3**	**3**		
• Average trip length *(km)*	**3**	**3**	**3**		
• Total income *(fl)*	814	407	204	7,735	1,137,052
• Operational cost *(fl)*	362	362	362	6,505	956,227
Bus					
• Passengers per leg	**50**	**25**	**10**		
• Number of legs per hour	**3**	**3**	**3**		
• Average trip length *(km)*	**3**	**3**	**3**		
• Total income *(fl)*	339	170	68	3,121	658,565
• Operational cost *(fl)*	217	217	217	3,903	823,526
Total					
• Income *(fl)*					1,795,616
• Costs *(fl)*					1,779,754

Note: Exogenous input values (rule of thumb) are shown in bold print.

This calculation shows a small profit of 1 %. Using the ratio between revenues per passenger kilometre and total income per passenger kilometre, the cost efficiency ratio becomes 32 %, which equals the cost efficiency ratio in the Annual report. Therefore, it is concluded that costs factors used in this analysis are realistic.

Two other remarks can be made with respect to this macro model:

- The number of legs per vehicle per hour is estimated assuming an average line length of 6 kilometres and an average speed of 20 kilometres per hour. Under these assumptions it is possible to make three legs per hour while allowing for some spare time per hour too.

- In the calculation it is assumed that all vehicles are used in all periods. Comparison of the calculated income per day and the actual income per year shows that the calculated income is twice as high. This implies that the average service period of a vehicle is not 16 hours per day, but about 8 hours per day.

Appendix C
Optimisation of variable stop spacing

The main design dilemma in the case of variable stop spacing is the balance between the travellers boarding and alighting and the through going travellers. More stops leads to shorter access and egress times but to longer travel times for travellers passing the study area. This dilemma will be illustrated for the case of optimising stop spacing D_s for the objective of minimising total costs. The line spacing D_l is assumed to be fixed.

Let us assume a small unit area for a given line with length D_u and width D_l. The number of passengers boarding in this unit area is P_b, the number of passengers alighting is P_a, and the number of through going travellers is P_t. Within the unit area the demand is uniformly distributed.

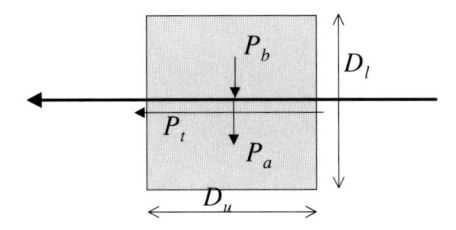

The access time equals the egress time and can be written as:

$$T_e = T_a = \frac{f_a \cdot (D_s + D_l)}{v_a} \tag{C-1}$$

where:
  f_a = routing factor for the actual access distance as a function of D_s and D_l
  v_a = access speed

The maximum speed and the time loss at stops due to decelerating, alighting, boarding and accelerating, determine the in-vehicle time within the unit area T_u:

$$T_u = \frac{D_u}{D_s} \cdot \left(\frac{D_s}{v} + T_s\right) \tag{C-2}$$

where:
  v = maximum speed
  T_s = time lost at stops

The total costs for the passengers boarding the line (C_b) are the access time plus half the in-vehicle time, multiplied by the value-of-time c_t:

$$C_b = P_b \cdot (w_a \cdot T_a + 0.5 \cdot T_u) \cdot c_t \tag{C-3}$$

The total costs for passengers alighting the line (C_a) are:

$$C_a = P_a \cdot (w_e \cdot T_e + 0.5 \cdot T_u) \cdot c_t \qquad \text{(C-4)}$$

The total costs for through-going passengers (C_t) are

$$C_t = P_t \cdot T_u \cdot c_t \qquad \text{(C-5)}$$

The operator's costs for this line can be formulated as:

$$C_o = c_o \cdot \frac{1000}{D_l} \cdot F \cdot T_u \cdot 2 \qquad \text{(C-6)}$$

where:
    c_o = operating costs per vehicle per hour
    F = frequency in vehicles per hour

The objective can then be written as:

$$MIN\{C_b + C_a + C_t + C_o\} \qquad \text{(C-7)}$$

Or more completely:

$$MIN \begin{Bmatrix} P_b \cdot (w_a \cdot T_a + 0.5 \cdot T_u) \cdot c_t + P_a \cdot (w_e \cdot T_e + 0.5 \cdot T_u) \cdot c_t + \\ P_t \cdot T_u \cdot c_t + c_o \cdot \dfrac{1000}{D_l} \cdot F \cdot T_u \cdot 2 \end{Bmatrix} \qquad \text{(C-8)}$$

The optimum for D_s can be found by setting the derivative with respect to D_s equal to zero:

$$D_s^* = \sqrt{\frac{\left(D_u \cdot (0.5 * P_b + 0.5 * P_a + P_t) \cdot T_s + \dfrac{c_o}{c_t} \cdot \dfrac{1000}{D_l} \cdot F \cdot T_s \cdot 2\right) \cdot v_a}{(P_b \cdot w_a + P_a \cdot w_e) \cdot f_a}} \qquad \text{(C-9)}$$

The following table presents an example of an urban corridor for two cases:
1. Uniform demand pattern, such as was assumed in the analyses in this report;
2. Variable demand pattern with, for instance, two shopping centres along the route.

In both cases the parameter values for the bus network presented in Table 7-1 have been used.

Appendices

The first case clearly shows the increase in stop spacing as the distance to the city centre decreases. Since there are no through going passengers in the city centre itself, the stop spacing decreases significantly. The resulting average stop spacing is nearly 550 metres, which is less than the 600 metres found in Chapter 7. In the case that the stop spacing within the city centre is ignored, the average stop spacing becomes 575 metres.

The second case illustrates how the stop spacing is influenced by concentrations of boarding and alighting passengers. Due to the travellers to the local shopping centres the average stop spacing drops to 450 metres.

Segment number (500 metres)	Uniform demand pattern			Variable demand pattern		
	In	Out	Stop spacing	In	Out	Stop spacing
1	25	-	483	40	-	387
2	25	-	503	40	-	412
3	25	-	523	45	-	412
4	25	-	542	25	50	396
5	25	-	560	40	-	447
6	25	-	578	40	-	469
7	25	-	595	45	-	463
8	25	-	611	25	50	444
9	25	-	628	25	-	628
10	25	-	643	25	-	643
11	-	250	254	-	250	254
Total/Average	250	250	538	350	100	450

List of symbols

Symbol	Unit	Explanation
c_o	fl/hr	Operating costs per vehicle per hour
c_t	fl/hr	Value of time for travellers
f_a		Routing factor for the actual access distance
f_c		Factor for the access distance perpendicular to a radial line
f_w		Factor for the waiting time
m		Transport mode other than public transport
n		Number of modes excluding public transport
r_s	fl	Subsidy paid by the authorities per traveller
r_{sk}	fl	Subsidy paid by the authorities per traveller per kilometre
r_t	fl	Fare paid by the traveller
r_{tk}	fl	Fare paid by the traveller per kilometre
v	m/s	Maximum speed of public transport vehicle
v_a	m/s	Access speed
v_{ax}	m/s	Access speed for access mode x
w_a		Weight factor for access time
w_e		Weight factor for egress time
w_w		Weight factor for waiting time
y_{xj}		Multiplier for weighted trip time element x and population j
B_o	fl/km^2	Operational budget for a square kilometre
C	fl/km^2	Total costs for travelling
C_o	fl/km^2	Operational costs
C_t	fl/km^2	Total traveller costs
D_a	m	Average access distance
D_c	m	Average trip length to the city centre
D_l	m	Line spacing
D_s	m	Stop spacing
F	veh/hr	Frequency
N_r		Number of radial lines in a radial city

Symbol	Unit	Explanation
O1		Objective 1: minimising weighted door-to-door travel time
O2		Objective 2: minimising weighted door-to-door travel time under a fixed budget
O3		Objective 3: maximising cost efficiency
O4		Objective 4: maximising profit
O5		Objective 5: maximising social welfare
O6		Objective 6: minimising total costs
O6.1		Objective 6: minimising total costs under the assumption of a variable level of demand
O6.2		Objective 6: minimising total costs under the assumption of a fixed level of demand
O7		Objective 7: maximising patronage
P		Level of public transport demand per square kilometre
P_0		Total transport demand per square kilometre
P_j		Population for e.g. trip type j or access mode j
P_l		Linear description of the relation between supply and demand
P_p		Level of public transport demand per square kilometre in reference situation
R	m	Radius of a radial city
R_o	fl/km^2	Total revenues for the operator
R_s	fl	Subsidy paid by the authorities
S_c	fl	Consumer surplus
T_a	s	Access time
T_c	s	Total weighted travel time to the city centre
$\hat{T}_c$	s	Weighted travel in reference situation
T_{cm}	s	Maximum travel time to the city centre where demand for public transport vanishes
T_e	s	Egress time
$\bar{T}_{et}$	s	Constant for the weighted egress time of city centre oriented trips and transfer penalties for transversal trips
T_i	s	In-vehicle time
T_m	s	Weighted travel time for mode m

Appendices

Symbol	Unit	Explanation
T_p	s	Travel time to city centre by private car
T_s	s	Time lost at stops
T_u	s	In-vehicle time within a unit area
T_w	s	Waiting time
α	min^{-1}	Coefficient for public transport in logit-model
α_m	min^{-1}	Coefficient for mode m in logit-model
β		Coefficient for travel-time-ratio
γ		Constant in travel-time-ratio model
ε	s	Constant in comparison of objectives O5 and O6.1
φ		Constant in logit-mode choice model for access mode 2
κ	s/m	Aggregate access factor
λ	s	Aggregate stop loss factor
μ	s	Fixed trip time elements
τ		Aggregate waiting time factor
ρ		Trade-off factor between traveller's and operator's costs
X_x^*		Optimum value for variable X_x
$\overline{X}_x$		Weighted average for variable X_x
$X_{x,i}$		Variable X_x for network level i

TRAIL Studies in Transportation Science

A series of The Netherlands TRAIL Research School for fundamental and theoretical studies on transport, infrastructure and logistics.

Kort, A.F. de, B. Heidergott, R.J. van Egmond, G. Hooghiemstra, *Train Movement Analysis at Railway Stations: Procedures & Evaluation of Wakob's Approach*, February 1999, TRAIL Studies in Transportation Science, S99/1, Delft University Press, The Netherlands

Egmond, R.J. van, *Railway capacity assessment, an algebraic approach,* July 1999, TRAIL Studies in Transportation Science, S99/2, Delft University Press, The Netherlands

Nes, R. van, *Design of multimodal transport systems. Setting the scene: Review of literature and basic concepts,* October 1999, TRAIL Studies in Transportation Science, S99/3, Delft University Press, The Netherlands

Heijden, R.E.C.M. van der, M. Wiethoff, *Automation of Car Driving. Exploring societal impacts and conditions*, December 1999, TRAIL Studies in Transportation Science, S99/4, Delft University Press, The Netherlands

Nes, R. van, *Optimal stop and line spacing for urban public transport networks. Analysis of objectives and implications for planning practice*, May 2000, TRAIL Studies in Transportation Science, S2000/1, Delft University Press, The Netherlands

Sales and distribution:
Delft University Press
P.O. Box 98
2600 MG Delft
Telephone: +31 (0)15 278 32 54
Telefax: +31 (0)15 278 16 61